Praise For

The Book of Easy Answers

This is a very relevant and important message to anyone who has ever grappled with real issues and deep questions of life. If you have pain, problems, and pathos, John and Kerry offer powerful and profound words of wisdom and a transformational message of help, healing, and hope for your hurts. In a heart-hitting and courageous way, they expertly yet compassionately tackle the toughest questions we can have as human creatures with their incisive reason derived from their grounded faith and years of experience in the ministry trenches. We need to develop a simple yet consistent faith, a yielded obedient attitude, and a humble but willing heart amid our agony, fear, and doubt. This excellent book will comfort your heart, challenge your mind, convict your attitudes, stretch your faith, and inspire your soul.

—**Jared Pingleton**, Psy.D., Clinical Psychologist and Minister, drpingleton.com, Author of *Making Magnificent Marriages* and Editor and Co-Author of *The Care and Counsel Bible, The Struggle is Real: How to Care for Mental and Relational Needs in the Church*, and five other books.

***

John Telman and Kerry Pocha take a practical and thoroughly Biblical approach in responding to some of the most vexing questions that humans have had since Adam and Eve vacated Eden. Life's great questions certainly invite complex answers and yet, in mining, God's word the authors help us see that by focusing on what we know of God and His ways, we can trust the unknown to a God who has made Himself and His will known. Both authors share their rich experience of walking with God through difficulty and complexity, leaving the reader encouraged and inspired. This is a book I'd recommend to anyone who is asking difficult questions.

—**Rev. Marvin Wojda**, Pastor, *Elim Church in Saskatoon, SK. Canada.*

***

John Telman and Kerry Pocha, have admirably written an up-to-date piece of work that carefully answers human dilemmas when trouble hits. The scriptural presentations in the book are coupled with real-life stories. This masterly work is a must-read for everyone.

—**Pastor Moffat Phiri**, International speaker, Founder and Senior pastor of the *Victory Christian Temple Church. Northern Malawi.*

***

What does it mean to have easy answers? It seems too good to be true to have a book that gives "easy answers" to life's troubles. I am married now for 23 years, and a mother of two boys. I work as a registered nurse, and, over the years as a wife, mother, and nurse, I have been faced with many difficult questions. "Why do bad things happen to good people?" "If God is so good, why do bad things happen in life?" "Why doesn't God heal me when I am sick?" Questions like these, and many others, have been asked to me and by me, and usually, my only answer is "I don't know," and my only conclusion is, "God is God, and I am not." What John and Kerry have accomplished in this book is to describe the simplicity of God's nature, and establish the fact that through our response to Him and His Word, we can have concise answers to life's biggest struggles. Does that mean that life itself is easy? No, not necessarily. The Bible does not promise us an easy life, but it does, however, give us instructions on how to live life easily. John and Kerry bring complex beliefs found in the Bible down to understandable concepts that one can use to navigate this life that is filled with uncertainty and perplexity.

This book beautifully describes God's character and how we can respond and partner with Him to go through life's troubles. In reading this book, I am inspired to grow in my spiritual journey and to know God on a deeper level. I find the chapters to be uplifting and encouraging. I recommend it to those who might be struggling to answer life's most diffi-

ii

cult questions, or just those who want to grow in their faith. This book is rich in wisdom to access the arsenal to defeat life's greatest battles.

—**Heidi Zimmerman**, Registered nurse in *general surgery, kidney dialysis, and transplant.*

∗∗∗

In an age of the internet "clickbait" and fake news, what we need is not more self-help or sensationalized supernaturalism, but practical truth presented clearly and engagingly. "The Book of Easy Answers" clearly lays out for every Christian the basis of the hope that we have in Christ, and how He is indeed all that we need in every situation. Through authentic anecdotes, sound exegesis, and an examination of historical and cultural contexts, John and Kerry show us how and why we should turn our head knowledge into true, simple, heart-converted faith. It is my honor to endorse "The Book of Easy Answers," and my pleasure to wholeheartedly recommend it as a resource for every believer who needs easy answers to life's difficult questions.

—**Elvin Foong**, Founder / Director, *The Treasure Box Singapore.*

∗∗∗

For the past two decades, I have met with and interviewed hundreds of followers of Jesus around the world who have suffered greatly because they were determined to serve God and spread the Gospel. What has impressed me is how many of them respond to persecution and how they are comforted by what God has to say to them through the Bible. They not only find answers to their questions concerning God's Word, but they apply the answers. I appreciate John's and Kerry's approach and insight in this book "The Book of Easy Answers." It is solid and practical. You will discover that we often find it hard to accept and put into practice the answers God has for us in our journey with him. My prayer is that this book will help you understand that God has given us all we need to navigate our lives and be content with his answers.

—**Greg Musselman**, Minister at Large *for The Voice of the Martyrs Canada.* Co-host, *100 Huntley Street TV program.*

***

There is no topic more important than theology (the study of God), including His character and attributes. This book is rich in real-life story and application and was very helpful during my difficult personal circumstance. It recognizes lament, not just pat answers, but 'easy' (not simplistic) ones rooted in Scripture (orthodoxy) and experience (orthopraxy). It will help the reader to be more like Jesus and less like Job's 'comforters.

For some, the problem of evil, suffering, and the mystery of God are barriers to belief and trust. While not a definitive treatise, the many helpful thoughts, Scriptures, and engaging anecdotes will benefit anyone and their sphere of influence. Timely and practical for these COVID times, written with a pastoral heart and theological clarity, it is a good investment of time and to give to others in their unique journeys. It personally helped me with acute, circumstantial stress, anxiety, and depression (SAD) leading to more joy and peace by the Spirit. The short read was timeless, refreshing in focus and practical principles, profound, and even providential.

—**William Huget,** Church elder and Advanced Care Paramedic.

The Book of Easy Answers

For the Questions You Wish You Didn't Have to Ask

John Telman,
Kerry Pocha

Published by KHARIS PUBLISHING, imprint of KHARIS MEDIA
LLC.

Copyright © 2021 John W. Telman, Kerry Pocha

ISBN-13: 978-1-63746-034-4

ISBN-10: 1-63746-034-1

Library of Congress Control Number:2021936511

Unless otherwise stated, all scriptural quotation is from the New American Standard Bible®, Copyright© 1960, 1962, 1963, 1968, 1971, 1972,
1973, 1975, 1977, 1995 by The Lockman Foundation. Used by permis-
sion.

All KHARIS PUBLISHING products are available at special quantity
discounts for bulk purchase for sales promotions, premiums, fund-
raising, and educational needs. For details, contact:

Kharis Media LLC
Tel: 1-479-599-8657
support@kharispublishing.com
www.kharispublishing.com

CONTENTS

Foreword

Jeff Hendred

The Book of Easy Answers is true to its title. Readers will find easy answers to difficulties we all face, such as the loss of a loved one, injustice or discrimination, and consequences from actions, to name a few. The problem is, although the answers are easy, they may be hard to embrace, because they are not the immediate or common reaction. For example, who would think that praising God would be the easy answer when you are the victim of injustice? How do you praise God when you have broken no law, yet are unjustifiably incarcerated? The answer is in the book. Indeed, every chapter is carefully written with the intent to remind (in some cases) and for others, introduce who God is, with the hope that one will trust God enough to have a personal relationship with Him.

Understand clearly, in no way, shape, or form are Dr. Telman and Mr. Pocha insinuating that problems don't exist. On the contrary, the more one reads, the more one learns about real-life experiences others, including the authors, have encountered. This is not your self-help, mind-over-matter recipe book. Rather, it is a book about real people, facing real problems bigger than any one person can handle alone. For that reason, if one is open, this is a book in which you will find these men pointing you to God, the Creator of the Universe, the One who is not limited in any way, the One who is greater than any problem you face on earth, and the One who has the appropriate approach to facing it... the easy answer.

The easy answers are in the book, the Bible. It is here where God provides the resources, we need to face our problems head-on and come out being the victor. Pocha and Telman do a fine job of pointing the reader to God by using the Bible as the source of reference. The easy-to-read Book of Easy Answers has chapters with which a reader can resonate, such as Pocha's chapters, *The Armour of God or "What do I do when everything is against me?* and, *The Fruit of The Spirit or "How can I go on?"* I found myself laughing and other times saying, "Ouch," as I related to the easy answers Pocha pointed out from the Bible: Do what you know is the right thing to do and stay connected to God (both paraphrased). These are answers right in front of us and easily accessible, yet we don't use them because they appear to be too easy, cliché, or we think we don't need them. It is when the problem hits us that we are often reminded of the easy answer we refused to heed. In some cases, such as written in these chapters, the answer is easy, yet our application is complicated or erroneous. It is in those times we don't see the answer being easy, and rather frustrate, or at times revert, to ineffective behaviors. The answer is easy and effective when applied appropriately. The authors make the application quite easy to understand and implement.

Jeff Hendred (EdS) is a native of Ottumwa, Iowa and is an elementary school principal in the Ottumwa Community School District. He is active in various civic and religious organizations that serve his community and the world. In addition, he is a small business owner and also serves his community as a lay minister. He is an amazing man who, through the years, has been modeling the way of respect, compassion, and faith to young people and families in the community. He was recognized for his efforts to improve his community with the prestigious Gene Schultz Community Service Award.

Introduction

John W. Telman

The title of this book may be curious and may cause one to question the legitimacy of its content. Life is difficult. The worst way to approach someone who is hurting would be to give them the flippant answer: Life is difficult. My mentor, Dr. George W. Westlake Jnr., often preached that he wished God would have given us "the Bible and a book of easy answers." So why would anyone write a book with the title, "The Book of Easy Answers?" In addition, does it seem presumptive to believe that easy answers exist?

Sometimes, there seem to be no answers at all. I recall going to a children's hospital the day after a terrible Christmas fire that took the life of a mother and three children. I met a grieving, inconsolable family. I was taken into a room to see the charred and bloated bodies of the deceased children. How was I, the family pastor, to answer the question: "Why?" The fact is, even though questions were being voiced amid tears and groans, the family was not looking for answers. At that moment, they needed a pastor who would weep with them and be with them when they could not possibly understand. Later, much later, answers would be sought, but would they be easy answers?

Pain is real and the answers often seem elusive, never mind easy.

In his book, *The Journey*, Alister McGrath disagrees with us. He states that, "There is no easy intellectual or emotional answer to suffering. But suffering is more than an intellectual game to be played by philosophers and logicians. It affects our emotions. Many who suffer feel abandoned by God. They feel that their faith has let them down. They feel the pain of confusion and bewilderment."[1]Respectfully, it could be that McGrath is asking the "why" question, whereas we are proposing the question, "who" as in, "Who is God in all this trouble?" Another question we suggest is, "What does this pain mean?" and finally, "How will God bring comfort?" But the most important question to ask when facing any problem is, "Who is God?"

The focus that we will be speaking of is our response, as opposed to seeking obvious reasons for the trouble. Sometimes, in all truth, we are wanting relief and not necessarily answers at all.

Casting Crowns recorded a song that says it well.

And I Will Praise You in This Storm©

I was sure by now God you would have reached down
And wiped our tears away,
Stepped in and saved the day.
But once again, I say amen
That it's still raining
As the thunder rolls
I barely hear your whisper through the rain
I'm with you
And as your mercy falls
I raise my hands and praise
The God who gives and takes away

And I'll praise you in this storm
And I will lift my hands
That you are who you are
No matter where I am
And every tear I've cried
You hold in your hand
You never left my side
And though my heart is torn
I will praise you in this storm

I remember when I stumbled in the wind
You heard my cry you raised me up again

---

[1] "The Journey," Alister McGrath, Random House Inc., 1999, p.131

My strength is almost gone how can I carry on
If I can't find you
And as the thunder rolls
I barely hear you whisper through the rain
I'm with you
And as your mercy falls
I raise my hands and praise
The God who gives and takes away.

(Mark Hall, Bernie Herms, 2006. Released by Beach Street and Reunion Records)

While reading the following pages, it will quickly become evident that there are easy answers. They are not frivolous or trite. Neither are they proposed as an excuse for ignorance. Answers are easy to life's questions because of who God is. That does not minimize the difficulties faced; rather it gives us a healthy perspective when we face trouble. The easy answers can be immediate, but often we first need time to grieve and ache but, in those times, we must also understand that we are not alone and that "troubles don't last always."

Mark Mittelberg writes that his four-year-old daughter took a tumble on hard concrete. Like a good dad, Mark ran to her side only to hear her say, "why"? His daughter Emma Jean asked several times, "Why? Why did this happen to me? but she really wasn't looking for an explanation. It wouldn't have helped her much if I had started explaining to her that she had on new shoes that were still rigid and not yet rounded on the front edges of their soles, making them more susceptible to catching the raised edges of the sidewalk, and that she therefore needed to pick up her feet a bit more when skipping down the sidewalk to prevent further incidents, and so on. That would have been an accurate description of why this happened to her, as well as what she could do to prevent it from recurring, even though it certainly wasn't what she was hoping for! That's because, in effect, she was verbalizing a question but really was crying out for help and comfort, which we immediately gave her in ample measure. This is a good picture of the situation of many people who are hurting and who almost reflexively raise the question "why?" My initial suggestion for addressing this topic is to realize that when your friends are experiencing pain they are probably not asking for explanations as much as they're looking for empathy, concern, and tangible expressions of love."[2]

Answers are not initially what we need when pain hits us, but there are answers when we are ready to look for them and receive them. The pursuit of easy answers is wise because they come from God. Since God can handle all that concerns us, His approach is best. All other potential ways to handle our pain have weaknesses, but God's answers are complete. They are perfect. They are strong.

The Psalmist wrote, "I look up to the mountains— does my help come from there? My help comes from the LORD, who made heaven and earth" (Psalm 121:1, 2). It may not feel like help comes from God. The truth is that I have spoken to many people who blame God for the trouble and pain they experience; they would not even consider God to be their help.

It is the premise of this book that easy answers are available if we would only consider who God is. The problem is that we may not desire the answers related to the person of God. Man's heart needs help. The good news is that there is help. My contention is that the help we need is not only available but is also deeply rooted in who God is. The easy answers presented will turn our attention to who God is. They are more than interesting bits of information. It is our hope that each chapter will drive the reader to not only know about God, but also to trust Him in a close, personal relationship.

In his monumental book, "Knowing God," J. I. Packer wrote, "…one can know a great deal about God without much knowledge of Him."[3] What follows are not just theological statements about God. By considering scripture and by recounting experiences in my twenty-six plus years of ministry in three countries, we will consider easy answers that draw us into that relationship with God, despite the pains felt. I will share the stories of real people, including Tony Dungy, Corrie Ten Boom, Steven Curtis Chapman, Joni Earekson, David Livingstone, and many others who have experienced dreadful trouble and have also experienced the help of God.

To live as if there are no problems is foolish. To avoid problems is difficult and sometimes creates problems of its own. The challenge is to turn one's

---

[2] "The Questions Christians Hope No One Will Ask," Mark Mittelberg, Tyndale House Publishers Inc., Colorado Springs: CO, 2010, p. 128-129

[3] "Knowing God," J. I. Packer, Evangelical Press: Welwyn Garden City, UK, 1993, p. 2.

attention from the trouble to God, who is our only hope.

My brother-in-law, evangelist and missionary, Mark Wicks, once reminded me that to fixate on problems is much like focusing on the lights of oncoming traffic at night. A driver who did so would be blinded and would likely drive into the light, much like bugs are attracted to light. To extend the analogy further would be to encourage us to keep our focus on God and not on the problem. Sadly, most feel unable to look away from the trouble, and the continued trouble seems to rule their lives.

The writer to the Hebrews stated, "Fix your eyes on Jesus, the author and finisher of our faith" (Hebrews 12:2). Of course, the inner eyes are implied, not the physical eyes. It is the inner focus that must be on God who is the only hope for everyone and in all situations.

The Psalmist David knew trouble. He had to run for his life on many occasions. He dealt with the pain of losing a child and the heart-wrenching struggles with family. He experienced dangers, anguish, hurt and yet he wrote, "The LORD is my shepherd; I have all that I need. He lets me rest in green meadows; he leads me beside peaceful streams. He renews my strength. He guides me along right paths, bringing honor to his name. Even when I walk through the darkest valley, I will not be afraid, for you are close beside me" (Psalm 23:1-4). David did not deny the existence of valleys but knew that God is not just the giver of easy answers. He is the easy answer to every trouble.

I understand some will not pick up this book because of the title. The fact you are reading this means you are hopeful of an answer of some kind. Your problem may not be mentioned but know that the problem is not the focus. God Almighty is the focus. The more we understand who God is, the more we rest in who He is, and the more we depend on His goodness, the more we will experience His help. Trouble may flee, only to return in another form, or trouble may just continue without seeming to end. Should there be no immediate change in your life, know that you are safe and cared for, even amid a terrible storm.

Hear me now: Trouble is not your answer to trouble! Anger is not the answer! Fear is not the answer. Unforgiveness is not the answer. In fact, anger, fear and unforgiveness are blocks to easy answers. They will create more troubles than they will solve.

God, through Jesus Christ, is your answer. He is the easy answer. As you read about Him in these pages and as you sense the One who loves you is near, I urge you to call upon His goodness and love. When you truly do, you will find easy answers. They may not be what you expect or necessarily wanted but they will be answers that will be the best. God makes the answers easy because nothing is too difficult for Him. If you're sick, He's the healer who is not limited by any disease or health issue. If you're in financial need, God is your supplier, because He is infinitely able to bring all the resources of heaven to help you. No matter what the problem is that needs an answer, God is not only your answer, He is your best solution. He is the only true solution.

When we experience pain, and trouble, we might say, "how could this happen?" There is a book in the Bible that is titled "how" in the Hebrew language. It is Lamentations, the 25th book of the Bible. In the Book of Lamentations, we read that the temple and Jerusalem were utterly destroyed by the Babylonians. Prophet Jeremiah understood that the Babylonians were God's tool for bringing judgment on Jerusalem (2600 years ago). Lamentations makes it clear that sin and rebellion were the causes of God's wrath being poured out (1:8-9; 4:13; 5:16). Jeremiah was known as the "weeping prophet" for his deep and abiding passion for his people and the city of Jerusalem (Lamentations 3:48-49). This same sorrow over the sins of the people and their rejection of God was expressed by Jesus. As was said earlier, some of our trouble is not of our doing, a great majority of the pain in our lives is a result of sin on our part, but God has not given up on you and me. He offers us life that is beyond trouble.

Billy Graham, the famed evangelist, wrote, "When I think about God's love, I tend to dwell upon all the good things He has done for me. But then I must stop and realize that even when circumstances have been hard or the way unclear, God has still surrounded me with His love. God's love is just as real and just as powerful in the darkness as it is in the light."[4]

As you read this book, see the greatness of God, and begin to engage your faith in who He is, and then watch as He simply answers with more love than you can imagine. You can begin to expect easy answers even as you read this book, since God really does have an answer for you. Instead of

---

[4] "Hope for Each Day," Billy Graham, Thomas Nelson Inc., Nashville TN, 2002.

becoming a close friend to pain and trouble, turn to the One who is infinitely able to bring easy answers. God is greater than anything that you are facing.

Answers may not be experienced easily, not because they don't exist, but for two important reasons: First, God may call us to the higher place of faith which will not seem easy to our emotions. This book will stretch the reader to place complete trust in God. Second, the answers could be staring us in the face, but we can't see them. Trouble often can blind us to the easy answers God has provided.

Kerry Pocha and I pray that as you read this book, you will gain courage to reach out to the Creator with faith. At that special moment, we are confident that you will receive an answer and it might well be easy.

As you will notice, Kerry and I have written individually but the theme of building faith in the One who has the answers threads its way through each chapter. Please consider the closing message to reach out to us with your prayer request. Together, we want to serve you by praying and believing for your easy answer.

Chapter One

The Joy of the Lord or "How Do I Find Joy in Trouble?"

John W. Telman

Smiles are not common. When photographs are taken, people are asked to smile. We are told that it takes less muscles to smile and yet smiles are infrequent.[5] In fact, we may be suspicious of people who are smiling. But smiling alone does not indicate that a person is joyful. Life can be filled with difficulties of various kinds, but a person can know joy simultaneously.

Joy is described as a fruit of the Spirit (Galatians 5:22) which means that joy is an outflow in life that comes from another source. In a later chapter, Kerry will look at joy as well as the other fruits of the Spirit, but let's consider joy on its own here.

The joy we are talking about "is a higher joy than just the thrill of an exciting experience or a wonderful set of circumstances. It is a joy that can abide and remain, even when circumstances seem terrible," writes David Guzik.[6] This may seem painless to write when life is going well but let's look at the lives of three people who experienced joy in the middle of great trouble.

The apostle Paul was a man who had his fair share of trouble. He outlines the numerous problems he faced in 1 Corinthians 11:24-28. Imagine! This man had been severely beaten numerous times. He told the church in Corinth that he was in danger in various ways. In fact, we often read that he was imprisoned. The ancient prisons were not like those of our day. Often,

---

[5] Numerous periodicals including The Washington Post, Dec. 1982, The New York Times, April 1987, The Denver Post, September 1998, give conflicting numbers but all agree that it takes less muscles to smile.

[6] http://www.blueletterbible.org/Comm/guzik_david/StudyGuide_Gal/Gal_5.cfm?a=1096 022

they were nothing more than a hole in the ground. In Paul's case, at times he was chained to guards after enduring a scourging (a horrible beating). In one incredible instance, we read that he and his friend Silas were finding an easy answer to their trouble (Acts 16:22-26). It was worshiping the Creator. That's right! Despite the problem, they began to sing their worship to God. They were strengthened even though they were still imprisoned and suffering.

All too often, we struggle with the issues of life by crying out to God, "why?" The problem is that an answer does not always change the situation. The "why" question may also be our frustration being voiced. "I don't understand" is commonly voiced by anyone who is hurting.

We also may struggle with the idea that God allowed the pain we experience but Paul and Silas didn't go there. Instead, they knew that the God they loved was worthy of worship, no matter what was happening. Amazingly, as they worshiped, they found superhuman strength! That's right! The joy of the LORD was their help to endure.

In another passage of scripture, we read that Paul prayed, prayed, and prayed again for God to take away a problem. The answer that he received from a loving God was, "my grace is sufficient for you" (2 Corinthians 12:9). The word that we translate to grace is the Greek word, *"charis"* which literally means God's help and His holy influence. We will talk more about God's help and holy influence in another chapter, but for now we see that Paul learned that right there, right in the middle of trouble, God gives help and His influence to go through the dark tunnel of trouble.

Worshiping God is appropriate always. Strength happens when we don't make much of the trouble and instead, we make more of God. As we focus on the beauty of who God is, we find His joy strengthening us.

It may seem strange to worship God while facing a mountain of problems, but both Job (Job 1:20) and King David (2 Samuel 12:20) stopped and worshiped God, regardless of the pain they were experiencing.

Alberta Wood, my aunt, tells of a remarkable experience she had after she endured the death of her only son. Dale died because of an accident when he was on a camping trip with his dad. It was pain of the worst kind for parents, but this was made worse since Dale was a wonderful boy. He loved people, including his sisters Christine (7 years old at the time), Heidi (10 months at the time) and his parents. He was a remarkable young man. Pain flooded Alberta's heart but one day, God pulled back the veil of Heaven to let her know that all was good. In fact, in a vision, she saw Dale and he said, "Hey mom, I made it."[7] This took place after she was encouraged by a pastor to praise God despite the sorrow and confusion. Prior to the healing of the heart, she worshiped. She truly abandoned her pain and just revelled in who God is. With peace invading her heart and mind, she later stated, "I knew without a doubt that Dale made it to heaven and was safe in a place where love, joy and peace resided. He was okay and suddenly I knew that I would be okay as well."[8]

Waiting for an answer is not easy. Conversely, worshiping God for who He is brings peace in the middle of trouble. It may be hard for our wills to choose worshiping God instead of grief and anxiety, but it is a powerful answer to trouble.

Ten-year-old Willie Myrick was in his front yard when a stranger kidnapped him. "He told me he didn't want to hear a word from me," Myrick said. That's when Myrick began to sing a gospel song called, *Every Praise*. The kidnapper started cursing and repeatedly told Myrick to shut up, but he wouldn't. He sang the song for about three hours until the kidnapper let him out of the car."[9] So, what were the words of the song he sang? Willie sang a song he had heard that was written by Hezekiah Walker:

Every Praise©

Every praise is to our God.
Every word of worship with one accord
Every praise every praise is to our God.
Sing hallelujah to our God
Glory hallelujah is due our God
Every praise every praise is to our God.

God my Savior
God my Healer
God my Deliverer

---

[7] "Intelligent Thought Management and The Thought Collector," Birdie Wood (2005) p.117

[8] Ibid.

[9] http://foxnewsinsider.com/2014/04/22/%E2%80%98every-praise%E2%80%99-kidnapper-releases-10-year-old-who-won%E2%80%99t-stop-singing-gospel-song

Yes He is, yes He is."[10]

Willie said, "I knew Jesus was with me and that He would take me through it."[11] Even at a young age, he learned to praise God. Even when he didn't understand what was happening, and even though it was frightening. Imagine what the kidnapper was hearing for three hours. "God my deliverer." What a wonderful witness to a man who was also in trouble.

Up until now, we have considered how we deal with pain and discomfort by worshiping, but in the book of Nehemiah we learn that worship is also the way to respond when confronted with the guilt of sin.

We must all admit that many problems must be the result of our actions and decisions. The Bible reminds us that all of us have basically told God to leave us alone. Every human being has wanted total control of their lives, which is sin. Some have even gone further in their atheistic view by encouraging others to "do what you want."

Baggett and Walls wrote, "God gives us enough freedom to make our choices culpable, but all of us go wrong and do so quite a lot, resulting in poignant feelings of moral failure. Those feelings, we submit, aren't illusory or imaginary; they are, at least sometimes, absolutely correct. They enable us to sense our short comings and to know that we need help. But a biblical portrait of reality reminds us that guilt is secondary; it's not our worst problem. The deeper problem is alienation from God, of which the guilt is but a symptom."[12]

One of my professors told me, "John, you have the right to be wrong." I believe this fact extends to everyone. The truth is, because there is only one Creator, consequences of rebellion result in trouble. Trouble extends to every part of this world. In other words, trouble is everywhere. If you're like me, you try to avoid it the best you possibly can. We also tend to avoid

---

[10] Hezekiah Walker, "Azusa the Next Generation," 2013, RCA Records.

[11] https://ca.video.search.yahoo.com/video/play;_ylt=A2KIo9r4wINTKlQAVRUWFQx.;_ylu=X3oDMTByYXI3cnIwBHNlYwNzcgRzbGsDdmlkBHZ0aWQDBGdwb3MDNA--?p=willie+myrick&vid=ddeab649af31a1798e0aeb0942e40f84&l=4%3A58&turl=http%3A%2F%2Fts2.mm.bing.net%2Fth%3Fid%3DVN.607989317110530109%26pid%3D15.1&rurl=http%3A%2F%2Fnews.yahoo.com%2Fvideo%2Fhezekiah-walker-willie-myrick-share-080144872cbs.html&tit=Hezekiah+Walker+%26+Willie+Myrick+Share+The+Life+Saving+Power+Of+Gospel&c=3&sigr=12i3et86r&sigt=125aca8vd&age=0&fr=yfp-t-715&tt=b

[12] "Good God," David Baggett and Jerry L. Walls, Oxford University Press, Oxford NY, 2011 p.189

our part in the trouble, but joy does not leave because trouble shows up.

When Ezra read from the ancient book of the law, people began to weep and mourn because of their sin (Nehemiah 8:9) but Israel was instructed that the joy of the Lord was their strength (Nehemiah 8:10).

No matter how we have messed up our lives, there comes a moment when the easy answer is to rejoice in the goodness of a forgiving and restoring God. He is in the business of fixing what we damage. The key is for us to worship Him no matter how destructive our decisions have been.

Joy, as such, is deeply connected to worship. We don't need to succumb to fear when trouble hits by our own doing or by some other reason.

Jesus called himself the "good shepherd" in John 10:11 and the writer of Hebrews calls Jesus Christ the Great Shepherd. God is described as the Shepherd of His People throughout the Old Testament. Psalm 23 reminds us that God, the Shepherd of His People, fully satisfies. "He let's me rest in meadows green." God, the Shepherd of His People, knows that His flock can be easily entangled by fear, so He leads them beside still waters. Since the Great Shepherd never leaves us, He is there to help us whenever we become discouraged and depressed.

The Psalmist one day was speaking to himself when he said, "Why are you cast down, O my soul? Hope in God!" (Psalm 42:11). We use the term, a "downcast face," meaning discouraged.

We've all been there. A downcast sheep falls on to his back out of fear. You may have seen scared sheep run and suddenly fall on their backs. We are somewhat like that. We may run and crash, falling in a defenseless position, but God restores my soul, so I rejoice in God my shepherd! That doesn't deny the problem, rather, it's a choice to approach it with joy instead of fear.

One last point to consider is that God is rejoicing. In fact, as we stated earlier, His joy is our strength. The infinite Creator and Sustainer of life rejoices. He rejoices! He doesn't rejoice in the destruction of the wicked, but He does rejoice, nonetheless.

A prophetic word came to Ezekiel and three times we read that God does not take pleasure or have joy in destruction. "Say to them, 'As surely as I live, declares the Sovereign LORD, I take no pleasure in the death of the wicked, but rather that they turn from their ways and live. Turn! Turn from your evil ways!" (Ezekiel 33:11). "Do I have any pleasure in the death of the wicked," declares the Lord GOD, "rather than that he should turn from his ways and live? (Ezekiel 18:23). "For I have no pleasure in the death of anyone who dies," declares the Lord GOD. "Therefore, repent and live" (Ezekiel 18:32).

So, what makes God happy? What is His joy that gives us strength in our troubles? Simply and to the point, God rejoices when we turn to Him in belief and seek relationship with Him. God has joy in us pursuing a vibrant relationship with Him. Someone may ask, "I am a Christian. I already have a relationship with God, so how is His joy helping me?" My answer comes from what I have observed in the lives of people.

Often, it has become apparent that people have become more of a friend to trouble than to God. What I mean is that sickness apparently becomes a close friend to some by how they speak. Have you ever heard someone refer to cancer or diabetes as "my cancer" or "my diabetes?" They know that it will be there when they wake up and they know it will not fail them, but God has great joy and that is our strength when we forsake trouble and pursue Him with our whole hearts. Do you see the tenderness and love of God? In the middle of difficulty, God's strength can help you to make it to the end. That strength is a result of relationship with God. Cancer is no friend. Diabetes is no friend, and whatever else you are facing is not a friend with the ability to bring life. Only God is your help. His joy will flood your life, no matter the circumstances. People will look at you and say things like, "What happened? They are still facing the same trouble but look how joyful they are."

I'm not suggesting that you smile through a problem, as if a smile alone will suffice. Rather, seek relationship with Almighty God, who is infinitely able to see you through the problem with joy on the way.

Someone once said, "Time heals all wounds." Nothing could be more inaccurate. Time is not a healer, otherwise there would be no cranky cold and indifferent people left in the world. Everyone would forgive because the pain would leave just because of time, but time does not heal. In fact, time may just harden anger, resentment, and unforgiveness into your life like concrete. Only God heals, and He wants to grant you joy; it's up to you to seek Him for His help.

Chapter Two

The Armour of God or "What do I do When Everything is Against me?"

Kerry Pocha

Many times in life we struggle with our difficulties. If you, like me, long to find an easy way to overcome these battles, then perhaps we should look at the defences God gives us as possible solutions to more easily winning these battles. Paul tells the Ephesians to use "the armour of God" in their invisible struggles "against the powers of this dark world."[13] There are two types of God's armour: The pieces we wear, and those we must wield. The boots, belt, helmet, and breastplate must be worn every day, while the sword and shield are generally carried until they are needed in a battle.

John and I have noticed that every piece of "the armour of God" (described in Ephesians 6:10-17) has been invaluable in our struggles, and either has an entire chapter to itself, such as peace, or recur throughout the book. Truth and salvation, for instance, are recurring themes.

Truth is a constant. It never changes. The apostle Paul referred to knowing the truth as a belt, or girdle. A Roman soldier's girdle was more than a belt. It was a skirt of armour protecting his upper thigh and groin. A solid hit to an unarmoured groin area will stop the strongest warrior. Every contact sport has a way of protecting this area, and a cut to the groin can sever the femoral artery, resulting in about a ten- to thirty-second death. The belt of truth is not a fashion statement, it is essential protection from anyone who would do you harm.

More than just protection, the belt ties together the other pieces of armour, and carries weaponry until they are needed. Everything depends on the truth. Every discussion, every thought we use to convince ourselves or others, depends on whether it is seen as true. Likewise, every piece of our

---

[13] Ephesians 6:10-17

7

spiritual armour either hangs off or is tied together by the truth. Especially our faith.

The shield was the most important piece of equipment to the Roman soldier when Paul wrote to the Ephesians. Without a shield, a fully armoured, highly trained soldier could be brought down by a simple, inexperienced archer from a great distance. In war this held true for thousands of years. Many countries conquered and held their land by the strength of their bows. Under a hail of arrows many armies failed to even reach their enemy's gates. Rome changed that with the invention of their large *scutum* (full shields) and formations such as *testudo* (Latin for tortoise). If the enemy were not careful, a Roman Century (an eighty-man heavy infantry company) could quickly close with their archers and decimate them.

Cassius Dio gives an account of a *testudo* put to good use by, the famous ancient Roman General, Marc Antony's men while on campaign in Armenia:

> "One day, when they fell into an ambush and were being struck by dense showers of arrows, [the legionaries] suddenly formed the *testudo* by joining their shields and rested their left knees on the ground. The barbarians... threw aside their bows, leaped from their horses, and drawing their daggers, came up close to put an end to them. At this the Romans sprang to their feet, extended their battle line... and confronting the foe face to face, fell upon them... and cut down great numbers."[14]

This is an example of how Rome put its shields and tactics to good use, but what I find more interesting than the shield is the tactics. Their soldiers worked as a unit. A single shield was useful, but a trained formation using them was formidable to the most hardened of armies. With experienced use, an army of Paul's day could close with the very gates of an enemy stronghold. Our enemy has strongholds and gates.[15] A unified church can overcome the enemy's gates.

We must remember that the Armour of God is Spiritual, and the apostle Paul describes our shield as one of made of faith.[16] This does not mean it is

---

[14] Retrieved April 2, 2015 from http://en.wikipedia.org/wiki/Roman_shield

[15] Matthew 16:16-18, 2 Corinthians 10:4

[16] Ephesians 6:16

ineffective, it simply means that we cannot see it. This should not concern followers of Christ since modern astrophysicists recognize that, of our universe, there is about 96% that surrounds us but cannot be detected by our most modern equipment. We simply see its effect and, for lack of a better name, call it "Dark Matter" and "Dark Energy." In his lecture series on The Inexplicable Universe, PhD astrophysicist Dr. Neil de Grasse Tyson states, "So, here's what you do. You take the energy contained in what we call 'Dark Energy' and it's 70% of all that drives the universe. Include with that percentage the 'Dark Matter,' and we are driven to the humble, mind blowing conclusion that 96% of all that is the universe is not anything we even remotely understand. Ninety six percent! And all our laws of physics, everything we know, love, interact with, and understand, or can even predict, anything about the future: that falls in the 4% that remains."[17]He later goes on to speak of quantum theory never being wrong until applied to the problem of this "Dark Energy." He says, "We put forth our best theory . . . to our biggest problem, and it gets us nowhere. In fact, it is the biggest mismatch between theory and observation that there ever was in the history of science." Dr. Tyson concludes, "So we are not only ignorant, our best theories in the universe can't guide us. So, I think that means we are driving blind."

"By faith we understand that the universe was formed at God's command, so that what is seen was not made out of what was visible" (Hebrews 11:3, NIV). Spiritual armour may be one of the simplest solutions to many of our problems, but we must use it, and that all starts with faith. But what is faith? The Bible says, "Now faith is confidence in what we hope for and assurance about what we do not see" (Hebrews 11:1, NIV). Faith is simply belief in action. So, what you believe is important. Any belief not based on the truth is based on a lie. The devil is known as the "father of lies."[18] A shield can only protect the bearer from one direction so if you are tricked into believing the enemy is attacking you from a different direction then you will point your shield away from the actual attack! So, before you can effectively use faith you must know and believe the truth.[19]

---

[17] Recommended Courses: The Inexplicable Universe with Neil deGrasse Tyson: "Inexplicable Space" 13/04/14. Netflix,
http://www.netflix.com/WiPlayer?movieid=70304282&trkid=3326038

[18] Satan is called "the father of lies," John 8:44

[19] 2 Thessalonians 2:13

So, what is the truth? Pilate asked Jesus that question just before he sent Jesus to His death. Jesus had already explained to His friends (the disciples) what the truth was. Jesus said, "I am the way, the truth, and the life" (John 14:6a NIV). Then He explained, "If you love me, keep my commands. And I will ask the Father, and he will give you another advocate to help you and be with you forever— the Spirit of truth. The world cannot accept him because it neither sees him nor knows him. But you know him, for he lives with you and will be in you" (John 14:15-17 NIV).

What? Why would Jesus exclude people such as Pilate from knowing the truth? Why should the truth be exclusively understood by those who follow Jesus the Christ? One of Jesus' disciples asked the same question.

> "Then Judas (not Judas Iscariot) said, 'But, Lord, why do you intend to show yourself to us and not to the world?' Jesus replied, 'Anyone who loves me will obey my teaching. My Father will love them, and we will come to them and make our home with them. Anyone who does not love me will not obey my teaching. These words you hear are not my own; they belong to the Father who sent me'" (John 14:22-24 NIV).

Faith in falsehood is foolishness, but faith in the truth leads to salvation.

Faith is simply acting on your beliefs, and any belief not based on the truth cannot protect us from the flaming arrows of the enemy in the invisible battle around us.[20] Roman soldiers encountered flaming arrows often, in their battles.[21,22] It is likely that the Roman soldiers of Biblical times prepared their shields to defend against flaming arrows by covering them in rawhide packed with vinegar-soaked seaweed or chaff [23] (apparently a more common practice during sieges on land or sea because of the added weight). To protect our souls from our enemy's burning assaults we must immerse ourselves in God every day.

Baptize comes from the Greek word *baptizo* and should not be confused with *bapto*. "The clearest example that shows the meaning of *baptizo* is a text

---

[20] Ephesians 6:16

[21] Retrieved March 11 2016 from http://classics.mit.edu/Browse/browse-Caesar.html, The Spanish Wars Ch. 11,12, The Civil Wars book 2 Ch. 2

[22] Retrieved March 11 2016 from
http://www.allempires.com/forum/forum_posts.asp?TID=19757

[23] Retrieved March 13 2016 from
https://en.wikipedia.org/wiki/Early_thermal_weapons#Defence_against_thermal_attack

from the Greek poet and physician Nicander, who lived about 200 B.C. It is a recipe for making pickles and is helpful because it uses both words. Nicander says that to make a pickle, the vegetable should first be "dipped" (*bapto*) into boiling water and then "baptized" (*baptizo*) in the vinegar solution. Both verbs concern the immersing of vegetables in a solution, but the first is temporary. The second, the act of baptizing the vegetable, produces a permanent change."[24]The Bible repeatedly tells us that followers of Jesus can, and should, be baptized in God's Holy Spirit.[25] Christians are baptized (*bapto*) in water, but are called to be baptized (*baptizo*) continually in the Holy Spirit. Our beliefs and actions must be soaked daily in God's Holy Spirit to effectively repel our enemy's attacks.

People do not become great at anything by believing that they can be great at it. They may start by believing that they can learn to be great, but they must act on their beliefs and practice. The quality of their training is what determines how much they will improve, and whether their potential is achieved. We must train ourselves to seek God's Holy Spirit daily.

"We do not rise to the level of our expectations. We fall to the level of our training." Archilochus, Greek Soldier, Poet, c. 650 BC[26]

It seems many of our next generation use fiction to determine what they believe. For instance, the helmet is often underestimated by modern youth as armour. When I have spoken to some who like to play violent video games, they have argued that a head shot is an instant kill in video games because it is realistic.

"If so," I ask them, "why wear a helmet in sports at all?"

"Because it is the law," they reply, "besides, sports are softer hits."

I reply, "Why would the government spend so much time and money policing helmets if they were not effective? And if you think they are only effective against blunt sport traumas then why would every army of the modern world spend so much money on equipping their soldiers with them? The answer is that they are effective in protecting soldiers from

---

[24] baptize. (n.d.) *Lumina Online Bible.* (2011). Retrieved September 13, 2016 from https://lumina.bible.org/bible/Acts+1.

[25] Matthew 3:11, Mark 1:8, Luke 3:16, John 1:33, Acts 1:5, 10:47, 11:16

[26] Retrieved from https://www.goodreads.com/quotes/387614-we-don-t-rise-to-the-level-of-our-expectations-we

injury and death."

So where are you in your journey? Often, we want an easy answer to our current pain, not how to avoid pain in the first place. When given advice on how to avoid repeated injuries, we simply roll our eyes and interrupt with a sarcastic comment such as, "Yeah, yeah. OK *MOM!* I know I should have worn my helmet. I'm an idiot. I know I shouldn't be skateboarding or doing anything fun." But, in my day, I (Kerry) have enjoyed many "extreme sports" and I've always found them to be more fun when I'm not injured. So, when learning any sport, I find someone whom I can trust to teach me a few things:

1. What is the safety gear?
2. How do I use the safety gear properly?
3. How do I fall (fail) safely?

Without all this information no sport can be played safely for long. Sooner or later, you will fall and if you do not have all the gear on correctly, then an injury (and the end of all the fun) is likely to follow. In nearly every sport, the first piece of safety gear anyone should find and never do without is a helmet. It is the easiest gear to wear and the most effective in protecting any player from serious, long-term injuries.

I have heard the church referred to as a "hospital for the spiritually sick and injured." If so, then a pastor is simply a nurse, and it would be silly for a nurse or a hospital to have a sign that reads, "All injuries are easily repaired here." Because of this, most preachers and teachers profess that there are no easy answers. So, why are John and I (Kerry) talking about easy answers? Because God neither makes His Will unknowable nor impossible to follow. Often, God's answers are so simple that we do not believe them. Most of God's answers are extremely easy to implement, as well, but they are only effective if used properly and pre-emptively. A helmet is of little use after a head injury has been incurred. An emergency room doctor may wonder why a motorcyclist was not wearing a helmet, but it will not help to ask the patient why they were not wearing one. Once the patient is stable and calm, then the subject of wearing helmets in the future could be broached.

The Bible has been described before by the acronym **B**asic **I**nstructions **B**efore **L**eaving **E**arth. God provided us a book of easy answers, but most of them are pre-emptive solutions. There is an old joke that reads: A man walks into a doctor's office and swinging his arm he tells the doctor, "Hey doc! It hurts whenever I move my arm like this." The Doctor looks at the man and replies, "Then don't do that!" Too often, I have found myself coming to God with a problem and essentially saying, "Hey, God! Someone gets hurt whenever I sin like this!" Then I am surprised when God's response is, "Then stop sinning!" Repentance (choosing to run toward God and away from the temptation to sin) is the first and easiest solution to most of our problems. When we repent, God has promised to save us from our sins (salvation). "Godly sorrow brings repentance that leads to salvation and leaves no regret, but worldly sorrow brings death" (2 Corinthians 7:10 NIV). So, "If we confess our sins, He is faithful and just to forgive us *our* sins and to cleanse us from all unrighteousness" (1 John 1:9 NKJV).

If you don't have a helmet, we have written a suggested prayer at the end of the book to attain one from God. You can flip there now, and God will provide you with salvation. If you already have one, then check it's firmly on your head. In other words, if you are not sure of your salvation, or if you know you have sin that you have not repented of then "STOP SINNING!" Get your head in the game! Any player who goes on the field without a helmet is simply begging for a head injury or for their coach to pull them off the field.

In all sports you need to "play heads-up." That means, while you're playing, you have to be aware of what is happening everywhere and at all times. Anyone in the game cannot remain in play long without a helmet. A Christian with unrepentant sins is just begging for the opposition to hit their head so hard they forget what team they're playing for, or even what their real name is.

> "He who has an ear, let him hear what the Spirit says to the churches. To him who overcomes I will give some of the hidden manna to eat. And I will give him a white stone, and on the stone a new name written which no one knows except him who receives *it*" (Revelation 2:17 NIV).

With salvation, our minds can be protected from enemy assaults. When we think thoughts that we are worthless, remembering that we are saved from hell can keep us "in the game."

John Telman says that it's ridiculous to think that any soldier would go into battle without the maximum protective gear in place. He told me that in our day of sophisticated weapons, an easy answer to danger is protection.

13

"Improvised explosive devices (IEDs), such as those used in the Middle East, are a challenging threat to US military forces. These blast weapons, often rigged to detonate conventional munitions such as artillery shells, have caused fatalities and severe injuries to Marines and soldiers. The introduction of the outer tactical vest (OTV) with soft armor to protect the upper torso against fragments, along with the ceramic small arms protective insert (SAPI) plates, has shifted the injury patterns sustained by Marines and soldiers."[27]

A quick look at the armour of God (Ephesians 6:10-17) helps us to see how important it is for a believer to be prepared for spiritual IEDs. God really does care for us, so we really can be adequately prepared for surprises that attack beyond the physical, but we must put on the armor every day.

Dr. David Jeremiah wrote this prayer for those Jesus followers who want to know how they can use God's armour daily:

Heavenly Father,
Your warrior prepares for battle
Today I claim the victory over Satan by putting on the whole armor of God!

I put on the GIRDLE of TRUTH!
May I stand firm in the truth of YOUR WORD so that I will not be a victim of Satan's lies.

I put on the BREASTPLATE of RIGHTEOUSNESS!
May it guard my heart from evil so I will remain pure and holy, protected under the blood of Jesus Christ.

I put on the SHOES of PEACE!
May I stand firm in the Good News of the Gospel so Your peace will shine through me and be a light to all I encounter.

I take the SHIELD of FAITH!
May I be ready for Satan's fiery darts of doubt, denial, and deceit so I will not be vulnerable to spiritual defeat.

I put on the HELMET of SALVATION!
May I keep my mind focused on YOU so that Satan will not have a stronghold on my thoughts.

---

[27] Retrieved May, 15 2015 from http://www.nrl.navy.mil/content_images/06FA3.pdf

I take the SWORD of the SPIRIT!

May the two-edged sword of YOUR WORD be ready in my hands so I can expose the tempting words of Satan.

By faith your warrior has put on the WHOLE armor of God! I am prepared to live this day in spiritual victory! Amen.[28]

Not only are they believers in a battle, but they also have help, an easy answer, for trouble of catastrophic proportions. The armor that he's talking about is spiritual because most of our troubles begin in the spirit. We cannot cure our illnesses by hiding their symptoms. Our troubles are most often symptoms of our broken relationship with God. Are you losing hope? Remember God's SALVATION! He saves us from the Hell we deserve and is preparing a place in Heaven for those He loves.[29] Do you sometimes wonder if God really has saved you?[30] Wrap yourself in the comfort of His TRUTH. God cannot lie. His promises are true forever. When you act on a truth you believe, rather than acting on a fear, that is courage, that is FAITH. So, raise your faith at every opposition, and it will snuff out the fiery[31] darts of Satan, which poison your thinking and cause you to fall. Are you afraid you might be fired? Remember the term came from the three managers who were thrown into the furnace for choosing to do what God wanted, rather than what the worldly powers demanded of them,[32] and be at PEACE. If God does not save you from the flame, He will stand with you in it. Persevere in doing RIGHT and remember, "Keep your lives free from the love of money and be satisfied with what you have. For God has said, "I will never leave you; I will never abandon you" (Hebrews 13:5).

---

[28] Retrieved January 22, 2017 from https://freedomfightersblog.com/2010/02/20/the-warriors-prayer/

[29] John 14:2,3

[30] Ephesians 2:8,9

[31] Fiery (from Hebrew Seraph) can mean poisonous since that is the sensation poison can cause. e.g., "Make a fiery serpent, and set it on a standard" Numbers 21:8 NASB vs "Make a replica of a poisonous snake and attach it to a pole" Numbers 21:8 NLT

[32] Daniel 3

Chapter Three

The Fruit of The Spirit or "How Can I go on?"

Kerry Pocha

But the Holy Spirit produces this kind of fruit in our lives: love, joy, peace, patience, kindness, goodness, faithfulness, gentleness, and self-control. There is no law against these things! Those who belong to Christ Jesus have nailed the passions and desires of their sinful nature to his cross and crucified them there. Since we are living by the Spirit, let us follow the Spirit's leading in every part of our lives. Let us not become conceited, or provoke one another, or be jealous of one another (Gal 5:22-26 NLT).

How is the fruit of the Spirit an answer to any question, let alone the tough questions of life? Well, why is this analogy even used? What is a fruit, where and how does it grow anyway? "Fruit is the name given to those plants that have an ovary used for food; vegetable is the name given to a large category of herbaceous plants with parts used for food."[33] So a fruit is a method used by plants to reproduce. The plant grows a flower on a central stem (or trunk or vine). This flower is fertilized through pollination, and the plant slowly transfers its resources into the fruit until it grows and ripens. Once ripe, the fruit is harvested from the plant or dropped to the ground by the plant to be harvested or grown there. A harvested fruit is eaten for the pleasure of its sweet flesh and the seeds are distributed by the harvester either intentionally or unintentionally.

John and I (Kerry) like apples. In Canada, it is too cold for most fruits to grow well, but we have abundant apple orchards in southern British Columbia, so I will use them as an example of a common fruit. All fruit is attached to a branch and the branch, in turn, is attached to the trunk of the

---

[33] Fruit(n.d.) *Farlex Trivia Dictionary*. (2011). Retrieved November 19 2015 from http://www.thefreedictionary.com/fruit

tree. If the fruit or branch becomes unattached to the tree for any reason, it ceases to grow. Though the fruit hangs from the branch, it is not the branch which grows the fruit. It is the tree which produces the fruit, because if we take the branch off the tree, then it will cease to grow any fruit. This occurs because the tree is the producer and distributor of all the nutrients it gathers from the air, rain, sun, and soil to the branches. The branch can get no nutrients from the soil or rain because it has no method to do so.[34] The branch is completely dependent on the trunk of the tree for the vital sap it requires not only to grow fruit, but also for its very survival.

If a branch is not well-attached to the trunk of the tree it will rip free when storms come. This is especially true of branches that have been grafted into the tree.[35] So the farmer must take steps to protect the branch; pruning of the branch is essential.

In the spring, each branch is examined for damage and damaged or diseased branches are cut off and destroyed. Branches that are growing too high or "proud" are cut low (or off entirely) so their fruit can easily be reached for the harvest.[36] Any branch that is growing inward or downward is also cut off because it will not produce large, healthy fruit. Good branches are also pruned so that they can become more fruitful. Some of these healthy branches may have to be cut back to half their length to ensure they will grow thick and strong enough to carry the fall harvest. The branches are then left to grow until they begin to produce fruit.

Jesus often used farming analogies. He warned his disciples that He would have to go away for a time, but that He would come back to them. Until He returned, Jesus promised the Holy Spirit, the Advocate whom the Father would send in Jesus' own name. Jesus then told His disciples this analogy:

"I am the true vine, and my Father is the gardener. He cuts off every branch in me that bears no fruit, while every branch that does bear fruit he prunes so that it will be even more fruitful. You are already clean because of the word I have spoken to you. Remain in me, as I also remain in you. No branch can bear fruit by itself; it must remain in the vine. Neither can you bear fruit unless you remain in me. I am the vine; you are the branches.

---

[34] John 15:4-9, John 6:56
[35] John 15:6, Romans 11:17-22
[36] Proverbs 16:18, 29:23, Leviticus 26:19, 2 Kings 19:22, Job20:6,7, Isaiah 2:11,17

If you remain in me and I in you, you will bear much fruit; apart from me you can do nothing. If you do not remain in me, you are like a branch that is thrown away and withers; such branches are picked up, thrown into the fire and burned. If you remain in me and my words remain in you, ask whatever you wish, and it will be done for you. This is to my Father's glory, that you bear much fruit, showing yourselves to be my disciples" (John 15:1-9 NIV).

An easy answer to many of our relational difficulties is for us to realize we are branches. If a branch is set in the earth it dies and rots. If a branch is attached to the tree it may suffer pruning, but it will live and grow and produce fruit for generations to come.[37] It is up to each of us to decide where we will grow. If we continually decide to be attached to the things of this world, we will die and rot, but if we attach ourselves to Jesus, then His Spirit will flow through us.

> "The seed which fell among the thorns, these are the ones who have heard, and as they go on their way they are choked with worries and riches and pleasures of this life, and bring no fruit to maturity. But the seed in the good soil, these are the ones who have heard the word in an honest and good heart, and hold it fast, and bear fruit with perseverance" (Luke 8:14,15 NASB).

I have never enjoyed being pruned. When I was young, our house burnt down (without insurance) and I have been knocked unconscious so many times I cannot remember them all. Perhaps this is a result of the head traumas, I don't know . . . sorry, what was I talking about? Oh yes, being pruned is not pleasant for the tree. Throughout my life I have been shunned, cast out, and rejected. My first wife left me as my business collapsed, and I went into a deep depression for years. I have battled with suicidal thoughts and have, literally, been told by loved ones to end it all; "to curse God and die." I have been poor and hungry. I have lost my father to cancer on my birthday in 2011, and too many other hard times to count or bother remembering. It is never easy going through hard times. Yet, even when I doubted God existed, even when I could not remember what His

---

[37] The last-known first-generation graft taken from the original McIntosh apple tree died in Ontario at 150 years old in 2011, retrieved October 25, 2015 from http://www.cbc.ca/news/canada/ottawa/oldest-mcintosh-apple-tree-descendant-cut-down-1.1001566

love felt like, and I longed for God to take me home, I reminded myself that my Saviour would be at the other end of the hard times waiting for me. This is known as RE-joicing. Taking a joy from the past and remembering it, is rejoicing.[38]

Throughout my hard times I kept on doing what I hoped God would want me to do, and eventually that became habitual. My habit of seeking God harder as my life gets harder has resulted in my grateful praises when the hard times fade. Now when I see more hard times coming, I relax, knowing that I will always love God and He can get me through anything. Paul wrote that perseverance, character, and hope grow through suffering.

> "…. And we boast in the hope of the glory of God. Not only so, but we also glory in our sufferings, because we know that suffering produces perseverance; perseverance, character; and character, hope" (Romans 5:2b-4 NIV).

When tragedy strikes, we may have to suffer a long time (and no matter how long it is it seems like a long time) and the Holy Spirit can give us the strength to do so, but it is through this that we are required to persevere so that we may gain the prizes of character and hope.

Unfortunately, when I read about the fruit of the Spirit, I often translate the words from their true, spiritual meaning into our common, modern interpretations of them. Love, for instance, has ten, or more, simple, yet different meanings. Love can be "a score of zero, as in tennis," sexual desire or activity, or even an object of enthusiasm (such as having a love of golf). Though the most common definition of love today is, "A strong feeling of affection and concern toward another person, as that arising from kinship or close friendship."[39] Really? Is our most sought-after emotion today simply a strong affection for a friend? Or can we agree with an old Funk and Wagnalls Dictionary which states:

> "Love is more intense, absorbing and tender than friendship, more intense, impulsive, and perhaps passionate than affection" . . . "Love of articles of food is better expressed by liking, as love, in its full sense, denotes something spiritual and reciprocal, such as can have no place in

---

[38] Read Philippians 4:4-9

[39] love. (n.d.) *American Heritage® Dictionary of the English Language, Fifth Edition.* (2011). Retrieved August 31 2016 from http://www.thefreedictionary.com/love.

connection with objects that minister merely to the senses."[40]

In recent years we have lost the "spiritual and reciprocal" nature of love. If we forget what it means for these fruits to be spiritual, we will be left with the impression that God produces the same fruit in us which we can receive from the world and others. Love becomes affection; joyful becomes happy; peaceful becomes agreeable; patient becomes permissive; kind becomes sympathetic; good becomes beneficial; faithful becomes trusting; gentle becomes submissive and being self-controlled becomes apathetic. As a result, worldly wisdom would tell us that to be Godly I should always be serene and never get upset or angry, or even really care what happens around me. When nothing bothers me, I just go along with everything, trusting that it will all work out for the best. This serenity assures me I am a good person when I sympathize with people's hardships and give to them the drippings of my success. Apathetically I can tolerate all kinds of actions without getting angry and simply agree to disagree. Then I will always be happy and my concern for others will only grow as they return my affections as friends.

Wow, that really sounds "guru" doesn't it? It even managed to get the idea of Karma, or "what goes around comes around" in there. It sounds so spiritual, even biblical, but it is a lie, and all lies come from the father of lies. This belief that we start being spiritual by controlling our emotions takes God's Holy Spirit out of command and puts us in charge.

The fruit of the Spirit begins with love, not friendship or affection, but God's sacrificial love for us, giving birth within us. True love is a fruit of God's spirit within us. Remember that "Fruit is the name given to those plants that have an ovary used for food." So, love, for instance, is not only birthed within us by God, but also will be used to nourish others. Fruit is not grown for the consumption of the branch; it is grown by the branch to distribute the tree's seed to the earth. Fruit must be sacrificed by the branch to be effective. The fruit of the Spirit begins with love, a sacrificial love, but it does not stop there.

A Christian loves Jesus so much because Jesus first loved and sacrificed so much for us. Our love for God's Son is true love. It is spiritual, reciprocal,

---

[40] love, Funk and Wagnalls New Practical Standard Dictionary, vol. 1 (New York: Funk and Wagnalls Company, 1951)

and sacrificial. That kind of love flowing into and through you gives rise to an almost inexplicable joy, an internal knowing that we are genuinely loved by Someone who knows us completely… Someone who found out our worst thoughts, motives and actions and still loved us unto death, and by His death bought us an eternal home with Him in Heaven. How can that not bring you joy?

God's joy blossoms into peace within our hearts despite the storms we face. This inner peace is based in knowing that no matter how bad it gets, or how often I've failed, there is Someone who loves me still, waiting with open arms at my home in Heaven. Inner peace gives rise to patience, and loving patience with others is kindness. For what is a kindness without love, but a selfish attempt to assuage some form of guilt or pride? It is simply Someone with superior gifts or resources sharing the drippings of excess with those in need with either a hope or expectation of gratitude. A kindness given with love, however, is an embrace of equals, and so it is with all of God's fruit. Patience without love is a lit fuse of tolerance. Peace becomes an armistice, an agreement to cease hostilities until each party is rested and rearmed, lest they are conquered by a third aggressor. Our concern for others may help us barter a truce agreement, but only when both parties learn to love one another will there be peace between them. Love is a requirement for God's fruit to be genuine, and "Love is more intense, absorbing and tender than friendship, more intense, impulsive, and perhaps passionate than affection."[41] Paul, the Apostle, wrote:

> "Love is patient, love is kind. It does not envy, it does not boast, it is not proud. It does not dishonour others, it is not self-seeking, it is not easily angered, it keeps no record of wrongs. Love does not delight in evil but rejoices with the truth. It always protects, always trusts, always hopes, always perseveres" (1 Corinthians 13:4-7 NIV).

It is this kind of love, like sap growing within us, that expands us until patience and kindness begin to pop out of us, like the soft, tiny golden leaves of spring. Each blossom of fruit is a promise of the tree to the branch that the tree's life will continue to flow through the branch and produce fruit. John Telman points out: "The Spirit of God does remarkable things in the lives of people who are abandoned to his working in their

---

[41] Love. Funk and Wagnalls New Practical Standard Dictionary, vol. 1 (New York: Funk and Wagnalls Company, 1951)

lives. In Galatians 5, the apostle Paul lists just what takes place when seeds are planted in lives that allow for the Spirit of God to work. No tree works to make fruit happen. It's a natural response to sunlight, soil, and rain. All three are out of the tree's control. The tree cannot make fruit happen. It just does.

"Translating this image to our lives, fruit, real fruit of patience, peace, joy, kindness, goodness, gentleness, faithfulness, self-control and love in the midst of trouble is something beyond us. How can a mother worship God with joy when her son has died in an accident? It's beyond her. God is the one who will bring these authentic happenings. What is our part? Surrender, submission, and humility. They will always, given room for God, do the miraculous in lives."

You see, it is not nearly so important what we do or even how we do it, but WHY we do it. Samuel the prophet was looking for the next king of Israel and had many mighty men to choose from, but God reminded him that, "People look at the outward appearance, but the LORD looks at the heart."[42] Others may look at what you did or how you did it and determine that you must have made a mistake based on the results, but God is only concerned with why you did it. Were you seeking to please God or yourself? Were you acting out of love or merely some personal concern? When you gave to a cause did you care more about how much was needed or how much would be left over for yourself?

It becomes easy to be at peace with people when we have forgiven all the wrongs, they've done to us. It is easy to be gentle with those we long to protect. It is easy to be self-controlled when you are not self-seeking. It is easy to have the fruit of the Spirit when God's Spirit of love flows through us. It builds within us and is trying to get out to the world around us. To have this kind of love in our lives we must get to know Jesus and His father, God. There is no other way, for God is love,[43] and it is His Spirit that produces His perfect love in us.

Knowing what fruit God is producing in us is an easy answer to why we should persevere and never give up in this fallen world. It also answers the questions we all have about how to have happy, healthy relationships with

---

[42] 1 Samuel 16:7
[43] 1 John 4:8,15-17

others. All we need to do is remain devoted to God and allow more and more of His love to flow into and through us to His fruit, and the world around us.

Chapter Four

The Grace of God or "What Help Is There for Me?"

John W. Telman

E
arlier, we introduced the Greek word that we translate "grace."[44] *Charis* is much more than unmerited favor. Grace, as is found in the New Testament, is God's help and holy influence in our lives. When faced with challenges and enormous trouble, it is more than comforting to know that God can and does help us.

For some of what we face, we certainly must take responsibility, but an accident or a health issue can be the result of nothing we did. In both cases we grapple with what to do. Maybe not today and maybe not even tomorrow, but it's a safe bet that, eventually, you and I will need help that transcends anything that Mom and Dad or a best friend can solve. We need help beyond what we can see or figure out with our limited human resources.

So, the two-prong blessing of God's grace, His *charis*, is an easy answer to whatever confronts you.

The Help of God

The help of God can come in many forms. If you're sick, God's help is healing. If your bank account is empty and there is no food in the cupboard, God's help comes through provision. My wife and I have experienced this kind of help too many times to count. God has the means of helping in ways that result in us saying, "I didn't see that coming."

When trouble comes, make it a habit to seek God for help. He is quick to listen and to help. It may be more convenient to pick up a phone and call a family member or friend, but their ability to help you is limited since they

---

[44] Sometimes *Charis* is also translated "favor". See Luke 1:28, 30

do not possess the resources that the Creator has at His disposal. What makes our problems pale is the reality of who God is. He is infinitely able to help. He's not just "nice" or sympathetic to our plight. He truly can help when we come to the end of our resources, and even before we add our resources.

In a later chapter, we will tell you the story of a man who was seconds from death caused by a cruel and horrible disease. To the friends and family of Bruce Merz, God proved to be greater than sickness. God alone could help when medical doctors were incapable of doing anything to help. The Creator is not limited in any way. His easy answer to your problem is grace. Here me now: God is your help.

He is your help for salvation. The apostle Paul wrote, "By grace (*charis*-God's help) you have been saved through faith; and not of yourselves, it is the gift of God; not as a result of works, so that no one may boast" (Ephesians 2:8, 9). The easy answer to eternity is God's help; there is no other way. You could try (and many sadly do) and will come up short, but God's grace is powerful and available for you if you will only place your faith in who He is. The apostle Paul also wrote, "The grace of God has appeared bringing salvation to all men" (Titus 2:11). Resist the urge to earn your way to Heaven; it is not possible for your efforts to be sufficient. Remember the words of Mary, the mother of Jesus when she said, "Oh, how my soul praises the Lord. How my spirit rejoices in God *my* Savior" (Luke 1:46, 47). Mary knew that she needed a Savior. She knew her need. She knew she needed help.

He is your help for your physical needs as well. What you need to sustain life and for what is needed when sickness comes, you will find in the grace of God. There are no physical needs that God cannot heal but you will often find that mankind is horribly limited. Doctors often confess that they can do no more to help when the body is sick. A wonderful friend and medical doctor, Alan Daniels, once said, "Doctors can cut but only God can heal." Let me share a personal experience to that point.

I noticed that I was not hearing well out of my left ear. When walking with my wife, she had to be on my right, so I could hear her well. After visiting my general practitioner, I was sent to a specialist. He did tests and told me that hearing in my left ear was markedly weaker than in my right ear. He sent me to a surgeon to see what could be done. Unfortunately for me, the surgeon, after checking the tests and doing his own tests, told me that there was nothing he could do. His announcement that I would lose total hearing was disappointing, but it did not shake me. My wife and I just went to prayer and did not worry about it. Obviously, mankind could not help but God could. During a graduate class, with my wife sitting on my left, my ear was dramatically healed. Suddenly, it sounded like the professor was screaming! My ability to hear him was nearly doubled. I had to see my doctor and the specialist. They needed to know that God could help me even though they could not. They tested my ear once again and asked when and where I had surgery to correct the problem. I told them that I didn't have surgery since the surgeon himself told me that it would do no good. The specialist told me something happened that he could not explain. The hearing in my left ear was now not only improved, but it also was better than in my right ear. He may not have had an explanation, but I did: God is my Charis healer. God is my help.[45]

Dependence on God for your physical needs is not only the best decision, but it is also the only way to exist. God has granted our bodies to function despite how we mistreat ourselves. The person who has abused his body with cigarettes and now struggles with emphysema has the grace of God as an easy answer. Gasping for the air that God grants is settling for less than what is available. God forgives, and He heals. Those lungs and those air passages can be made new by the grace of God. It won't just be a physical change, but it will also be a change to the mind and heart of the one who calls on the name of the LORD.

Jesus forgave a woman caught in the very act of adultery. When He restored her life He said, "Go and sin no more" (John 8:11). God not only helps us through the problem, but He also influences our lives so that we will be pleasing to Him. Think about it for a moment: This woman now had the grace (*charis*- God's help and influence) of God to make it possible not to sin.

The person who is healed from emphysema doesn't return to smoking does he? The way he lives now is with the help and influence of God. That is powerful help. Although addictions can be overwhelming, I want you to know that God is more powerful! You are not alone. You don't fight the

---

[45] I have the report of the specialist where he could not explain the healing that took place.

things of your past on your own. God is with you and loves you, so you have His amazing help to change your life. Why settle for so little when the Creator is waiting for you to commit your life to Him. When you trust Him with your decisions, He will strengthen you in ways that will change your life. The key to receiving God's help is to humble ourselves and admit to God, and ourselves, that we need His help.

The Influence of God

Since we all struggle with what to do in this life, we are in desperate need of God's holy influence. It's up to us to respond to this influence. When we feel the heat of the day, we are influenced to protect ourselves from the heat by drinking a cool glass of lemonade and shedding layers of clothing. When trouble comes in its disastrous ways, we want to be influenced by God and not the destructive forces of fleshly ways and worldly desires. After all, they may come in direct opposition to God's way, which is life and peace.

All too often we witness people being influenced by a problem and not by God. When frustrated, a man might lash out in a violent act. When tempted with the prospect of illegally making money, someone might cause much pain and heartache by selling drugs. Daily, there are stories of people being influenced by tension and reacting with what is now known as "road rage."

Who or what is influencing your life? Is it envy? Is it fear? Is it hatred? During one twenty-four-hour period, a person will have dozens of influences that can lead to devastation. God desires to influence you so that you will have life, real life, right now.

The grace of God not only helps us, but it also influences us to act in love and with kindness. The answer to trouble is not creating more trouble by letting the original problem direct our response.

In the book, *Higher Principle Living*, E. Garry Foreman wrote:

> "What should we do when confronted by circumstances that demand a personal or corporate response? We can all make the claim that we stand on principle. That is commendable. But we must always ask if we are standing on the highest principle—the principle of love. You must decide on every occasion whether you have prioritized to the highest principle of redemptive love, or if you have taken your stand on good,

legitimate but LOWER principles."[46]

God's influence is directing towards life and not condemnation. If we will be more influenced by God than we are a problem, we will act in love. This love will overlook a wrong. It will win with kindness. Sadly, we don't often see this. Rather, we see "eye for eye" retribution. God loves everyone, so He wants to heal and create life through you and me. His influence does not condemn and destroy.

Have you ever heard that "still, small voice" speak to you about your response to a problem or to an irritant? The apostle Paul wrote that there is help. "As many as are led by the Spirit of God, these are sons[47] of God. For you did not receive the spirit of bondage again to fear, but you received the Spirit of adoption by whom we cry out, 'Abba, Father.' The Spirit Himself bears witness with our spirit that we are children of God, and if children, then heirs; heirs of God and joint heirs with Christ, if indeed we suffer with Him, that we may also be glorified together" (Rom 8:14-17).

The influence of God is for life, not for death. He is the creator who made all. He seeks to give healing and to redeem every person, including you and me. Any time you encounter the urge to lash out in a destructive way, understand that you are not being influenced by God. It's at that point we are wise to ask not only for God's help, but also for His influence. This may seem unfair, but it leads to life and worse problems are avoided.

God knows better what our "next move" should be for life and health. Listening to His promptings and following His design for our lives will surely take us through the difficulties of life, no matter what they might be.

Pilots flying in a storm or in darkness become disoriented and are even deceived by their own senses. They can even be circling when their senses tell them they are going in a straight line. To keep flying safely they must rely on the instruments in the plane. Those instruments will tell the pilot what is actually and true. As we enter dark times, God guides us when we may be led astray by our own thoughts and passions. Later we will look at the wisdom of God to help us. For now, understand that the grace of God, His *charis*, His holy help and influence, will see you through the problems

---

[46] Higher Principle Living: A Call to Redemptive Leadership, E. Garry Foreman, WorldCom: Mississauga, ON, 2014, p. 22

[47] Sons here is a legal term which includes male and female

that seem insurmountable.

The grace of God has largely been viewed as God winking at our sin. It's not! His grace results in growth and stability in our lives. We handle trouble with serenity. God's grace is far more powerful than anything you will face. Don't doubt but invite the Creator to prove His amazing grace. As you do so, you will be able to join the apostle Paul when he wrote, "We praise God for the glorious grace he has poured out on us who belong to his dear Son" (Ephesians 1:6).

Chapter Five

The King of the Kingdom or "What's With all the Evil?"

Kerry Pocha

A s I prepared to write this chapter, John pointed out, "The rule of despot is what many fear. Rulers often do not care if their own people are hurt or even killed. Horrible examples dot history. Pol Pot, Hitler, Amin, Hussein, and many others selfishly ruled with no regard for people." So, we must ask ourselves some questions: "Who is the King of Heaven. Is He a despot to be overthrown? What is His power and what is His Kingdom? Is there another ruler I can follow?" Well, I will deal with the power of God in another chapter. For now, let's just look at God's Kingdom and if there is another ruler I can follow.

In the Gospel of Matthew, the Bible speaks of two rulers and three spiritual kingdoms. These kingdoms are:

1. The kingdom of the world (or earthly kingdoms).[48]
2. The kingdom of heaven.[49]
3. The kingdom of God.[50]

Before we go any further, I am going to ask the question, "Is there a difference between the kingdom of Heaven and the kingdom of God?" Well, it seems they are the same, yet different.

Kenneth E. Bailey wrote, when discussing the Beatitudes, "But what precisely is the kingdom of God? There is no simple answer to this question."[51] He then went on to write that "Many people at the time of Jesus used the phrase *the kingdom of God* to describe a Jewish state where

---

[48] Matthew 4:8

[49] Matthew 4:17, 5:3, 5:10, 19, 7:21, 8:11, 10:7, 11:11,12, 12:12, 13:11,24,31,33.

[50] Matthew 12:28, 19:24, 21:31, 43

[51] "Jesus Through Middle Eastern Eyes," Kenneth E. Bailey, Inter Varsity Press, 2008, p. 69.

God alone was King."[52] Jesus, apparently, liked to play with words. He often had interesting word battles with the Pharisees of His day. When He spoke, His words were carefully chosen to have a parable, a second parallel meaning that may not easily or immediately be understood by those present. By doing so, He could make a factual statement while illustrating a deeper truth. Jesus' genius is again demonstrated with His use of the term, "kingdom of God." Though the scholars of the day thought God's kingdom to be a physical locale on earth at His crucifixion, Jesus told Pilate plainly, "My kingdom is not of this world. If My kingdom were of this world, My servants would fight, so that I should not be delivered to the Jews; but now My kingdom is not from here." Pilate therefore said to Him, "Are You a king then?" Jesus answered, "You say *rightly* that I am a king. For this cause I was born, and for this cause I have come into the world, that I should bear witness to the truth. Everyone who is of the truth hears My voice" (John 18:36,37 NKJV).

Jesus' Kingdom is more than a physical territory to be seen and experienced empirically, but like physical kingdoms, it must first be found and fought for in the hearts and minds of those who long to see it.[53]

Heaven is where God resides, but His Kingdom extends beyond there. It is everywhere, and nowhere. It is the territory that He has, does, and will one day rule. But most importantly, it is everything He is allowed by believers to have kingship over.

For instance, Canada is a place where trees, mountains, lakes, its people, Prime Minister etc. . . . reside, but there are also Canadians who live in and visit foreign countries. Canada has embassies in many other countries. These embassies are considered Canadian soil and are there to help Canadian citizens inform and influence other people about Canada. Embassies can help people enter Canada for a visit or aid them to become citizens.

Christians are called ambassadors for Christ[54] and often our churches work as embassies for God's Kingdom. This was commonly understood in the past when people could run into a church and claim sanctuary just as they

---

[52] "Jesus Through Middles Eastern Eyes," Kenneth E. Bailey, Inter Varsity Press, 2008), p. 69, cited "The Zealots," Martin Hengel, (Edinburgh: T & T Clark, 1989) pp. 91-94.

[53] Matthew 11:12

[54] 2 Corinthians 5:20

could in any embassy. It seems to me that the Kingdoms of Heaven and of God are like a country and its embassies. Heaven is where God lives, rules, and sits on His throne.[55] Those who call God their King are His ambassadors. We may live on earth, but this is a temporary assignment. We are here to tell people about God's Kingdom and help them learn how to become citizens. An ambassador works diligently. Even though they do not know when they may be called home, they are glad when they get to go home. They are glad because they know that all the things they have used in the foreign country are not theirs. They are on loan from their king and country. They may have big cars and enjoy diplomatic immunity as ambassadors, but what good king would not give them as much and more when they return home after faithfully serving overseas? Christians know their king is VERY good. He created this entire universe in seven days, yet when Jesus rose to Heaven, He said that He was going to prepare our homes in Heaven.[56] That was over seven hundred thousand days ago! The Kingdom of Heaven is going to be that much greater than the earth He created here.

Sadly, not everyone knows the sovereign God of the Bible as good. They believe that if there is a larger power in charge of the world, it does not like them. They view this world, the condition it is in, and have determined that its ruler is a despot who needs to be overthrown. They are then told, by well meaning Christians, that "Bible God" is sovereign over all. Their conclusion is to blame "Bible God" for all the evil in the world. I have heard scoffers say that Heaven is not worth fighting for. They say, "It must be boring to live for eternity on clouds, playing harps and being God's butler or chambermaid." The same philosophers have said that they "would rather go to hell, since that is where all my friends will be." Here is a quote from one such philosopher: "Would hell really be such a bad place? Would I really want to be around Bible god for all eternity? He is such an [@$$#%!&]. I mean we all know how he is. I don't think I need to elaborate. There is no telling how he might flip on you once you get past the pearly gates. In fact, I think it would be worse being stuck under him. You would have to mind your Ps and Qs like an abused foster child. So, I think hell would be better. There will be so many great people in hell as

---

[55] Matthew 5:34, Isaiah 66:1
[56] John 14:2,3

well. A lot of rock stars, gay people, Ghandi, Buddha, The Dalai Lama, and the list goes on and on. There would be so much to do in hell. To me hell would be a lot more fun...And if we buy a state-of-the-art air conditioner it will be even better."[57] (curse words replaced by author).

As we can see, God does not choose to send anyone to hell. They choose to be lured there by "the father of lies,"[58] They have, unfortunately, mistaken Satan, the ruler and god of this material world, as "Bible God", who is the King of all. They are right about one thing, though, there is a despot in charge who needs to be overthrown.

When I say that "Bible God" is King of all, but He is not the ruler of this material world[59] I am not contradicting myself. The Bible is clear that God owns this world, and all that is in it, but He put us (humanity) in charge. Sadly, when Adam and Eve, the first humans, chose to disobey God, they passed the keys of this worldly kingdom over to Satan and he has been dangling them in front of each of us ever since. Even Jesus was tempted by Satan's power over this world: "Again, the devil took him to a very high mountain and showed him all the kingdoms of the world and their splendour. 'All this I will give you,' he said, 'if you will bow down and worship me.' Jesus said to him, 'Away from me, Satan! For it is written: "Worship the Lord your God and serve him only"'" (Matthew 4:8-10, NIV).

When Adam and Eve first disobeyed God, mankind was infected by something like a disease, or a genetic disorder which is passed along our bloodlines to all our children. This "disease" causes all sorts of problems daily, and it is painful to live with. The diagnosis is terminal. It is called sin. We are born with it. We are not sinners because we sin, we sin because we are born as sinners.

When a mother gives birth to a child an eternal being is created. This child's soul shall live forever even as its body grows old and dies. This new soul, however, is infected with the disease of sin. The soul wants to live, but unless a cure is given, the soul can only survive in its biological suit. Many souls are tricked by Satan into believing that this suit, this life, is all that is

---

[57] Retrieved February 23, 2017 from http://www.ex-christian.net/topic/8990-i-think-i-would-rather-be-in-hell/

[58] Satan is called "the father of lies," John 8:44

[59] Satan is called the prince, or ruler of this world; John 12:31, 14:30, 16:11, 2 Corinthians 4:4, Ephesians 2:2, 1 John 4:4, 5:19

worth fighting for. God, however, loves humanity so much that "He gave his Son, his one and only Son, and this is why: So that no one need be destroyed; by believing in him, anyone can have a whole and lasting life. God didn't go to all the trouble of sending his Son merely to point an accusing finger, telling the world how bad it was. He came to help, to put the world right again. Anyone who trusts in him is acquitted; anyone who refuses to trust him has long since been under the death sentence without knowing it. And why? Because of that person's failure to believe in the one-of-a-kind Son of God when introduced to him" (John3:16a-18, The Message).

When our "bio-suits" fail, there are only two places to go: Either the sin-free Kingdom of Heaven or the "quarantined zone" of hell. By believing in Jesus as God's One and Only Son we have access to the inoculation of our terminal disease.[60] When we choose to live our lives based on this belief, it changes everything. Our souls are healed and will live forever. Our bio-suit is no longer required to sustain us, it becomes a hindrance. Our lives would be so much easier if we were free to walk about as our true, God-saved, sin-free selves, unencumbered by the bio-suit's ponderous bulk. Until God takes us to Heaven, we go about out lives in this world, tripping, fighting, and stumbling in our flesh as other souls, still dependent upon their bio-suits, laugh and call us fools for not spending our time on earth trying to keep our bio-suit safe and comfortable. While we spend our time and resources helping ourselves and others get clearer pictures of eternal things, things our souls will enjoy for eternity, those souls still trapped in their costumes of flesh purposely ignore the fact that these bio-suits are aging and will one day . . . fail. They need an eternal solution. They need an inoculation that can only be given by the King of God's Kingdom . . . Jesus.

The easy answer to why there is evil in this world and what we can do about it is that "this world" is ruled by a usurper. Do not be confused by the labyrinth of religions out there. There is only one ruler, one usurper of this world, Satan, who offers nothing but worldly wealth and "the tranquility of servitude." He is "the father of lies," and the contaminator of our souls. His kingdom, however, shall not stand forever. As in the formation of the United States of America, a revolution is coming, when Satan shall be

---

[60] John 3:18, 1 John 1:7,9, Hebrews 9:14, Revelation 1:5

overthrown for a thousand years[61] and then forever. Samuel Adams told fellow revolutionaries: "If you love wealth greater than liberty, the tranquility of servitude greater than the animating contest for freedom, go home from us in peace. We seek not your counsel, nor your arms. Crouch down and lick the hand that feeds you; May your chains set lightly upon you, and may posterity forget that you were our countrymen."[62]

Two of the greatest desires we get trapped by are those of wealth and tranquility. "If only I had a little more stuff to cushion the blows," or, "If only I did not have to constantly fight for what I believe…" these thoughts and the attempts to attain wealth and tranquility divert our attention from the oppression of the usurper. We are tricked into giving up our freedoms to attain a little peace of mind. Benjamin Franklin warned, "They who can give up essential liberty to obtain a little temporary safety deserve neither liberty nor safety."[63]

We must stand firm then, in the knowledge that though our souls be free, we remain in enemy-occupied territory. Often, we are surrounded: "We are hard pressed on every side, but not crushed; perplexed, but not in despair; persecuted, but not abandoned; struck down, but not destroyed" (2 Corinthians 4:8,9 NIV). As the apostle Paul said: "It is for freedom that Christ has set us free. Stand firm, then, and do not let yourselves be burdened again by a yoke of slavery" (Galatians 5:1 NIV).

The usurper knows he is immortal, so he will never give up trying to chain us to the desires of this momentary world. We forget that we are immortal beings wearing a disposable smock and we grow weary. We see the muck our foe throws upon us and think, "Why keep on keeping on? What choice is there?" We must agree with America's founding father, George Washington, who fought for a country, envisioned in heart and mind, yet unseen when he penned these words: "Our cruel and unrelenting Enemy leaves us no choice but a brave resistance, or the most abject submission; this is all we can expect - We have therefore to resolve to conquer or die: Our own Country's Honor, all call upon us for a vigorous and manly exertion, and if we now shamefully fail, we shall become infamous to the

---

[61] Revelation 20:1-7,10

[62] Retrieved December 9, 2016 from http://www.azquotes.com/author/99-Samuel_Adams

[63] Retrieved December 9, 2016 from
https://www.goodreads.com/author/show/289513.Benjamin_Franklin

whole world. Let us therefore rely upon the goodness of the Cause, and the aid of the supreme Being, in whose hands Victory is, to animate and encourage us to great and noble Actions - The Eyes of all our Countrymen are now upon us, and we shall have their blessings, and praises, if happily we are the instruments of saving them from the Tyranny meditated against them. Let us therefore animate and encourage each other, and shew the whole world, that a Freeman contending for Liberty on his own ground is superior to any slavish mercenary on earth."[64]

Followers of Christ know they are freemen and their ground, their very souls, are owned by God alone. Though the usurper rail against us, may we continue to fight for our King, our freedom, and our fellow countrymen as vehemently as America fought for its Liberty. "Therefore, we do not lose heart. Though outwardly we are wasting away, yet inwardly we are being renewed day by day. For our light and momentary troubles are achieving for us an eternal glory that far outweighs them all. So, we fix our eyes not on what is seen, but on what is unseen, since what is seen is temporary, but what is unseen is eternal" (2 Corinthians 4:16-18, NIV).

---

[64] Retrieved December 10, 2016 https://www.goodreads.com/quotes/136607-our-cruel-and-unrelenting-enemy-leaves-us-no-choice-but

Chapter Six

The Mercy and Justice of God or "Why is Life so Unfair?"

Kerry Pocha

When we are in trouble it is easy to find someone or something to blame as the cause of our pain. When we cannot find someone, we look at God and blame Him. Why? Because if we can blame another, then we can demand justice. If we cannot find another to blame, there is only one person left to blame . . . ourselves. If we are to blame, then justice demands that we have to pay the price and we are already paying too much. Don't I get credit for all the times I did something good without being repaid or when someone did something wrong to ME without getting paid back? It seems that when things go wrong, we want justice for every wrong ever done to us and mercy for every wrong we have done, but the opposite seems to be happening. Why is life so unfair?

Mercy can only be given when justice is imminent. When we ask for mercy, it can only come from someone in power who is able to punish us for something, we have done wrong. If we have not done anything wrong and we are about to be punished then we do not need mercy, though we may want to beg for it; no, we want justice. We want the wrongdoers to be punished and we, who are doing right, to be praised. Mercy is what the wrongdoers about to be punished need to beg for. Justice is what the righteous about to be punished cry out for.

Let me give an example. One time, years ago, I was in enrolled in an engineering, graphics and design course. I had to design and draw a house in one of the classes and I decided to spend a little extra time and effort so I might use the finished product as part of my resumé. Soon after I submitted my work I was summoned into the professor's office. Since I was at the top of my class I was not concerned, but when I arrived, the dean and several professors were waiting for me. I was informed that my work was nearly identical to another student's work. One of us was obviously cheating. The other student was in jeopardy of failing several courses and had wiped the memory of my programmable calculator just prior to our finals, so it was clear who was the main suspect. The school had no choice, however. Without proof of who the original author of the work was, we would BOTH be failed. I already had job offers from architectural and engineering firms after I graduated, but that was now in danger of being postponed by a year, if not lost entirely. I was about to be punished for something I did not do. Did I ask for mercy? NO! I wanted justice. Mercy is what the other guy needed.

You may be able to relate a similar story. Why do such things occur? Well, I explain in the kingdom chapter that humans have given control of this world to the usurper, Satan. Satan is NOT just. He opposes the incarnation of justice. Satan wants this world to be unjust, because if it were fair and just, then he would be the first to be punished. Now if you were in Satan's position, you would know that a fall-guy for all this injustice is necessary. So, who do you get? Well, obviously, God is Satan's enemy so he would try to lay the blame on Him. So how do you get people to blame the author of justice for being unjust? It's like blaming water for our thirst!

The Greek philosopher Epicurus posed an argument against the existence of God (which was also cited by modern philosopher David Hume). It is as follows:

1. If God is willing to prevent evil but is not able to then He is not omnipotent.
2. If He is able, but not willing then He is malevolent.
3. If He is both able and willing, then why does evil exist?
4. If He is neither able nor willing, then why call Him God?

These philosophers argued that if God were good and just, He would not tolerate evil, and since there is obvious evil in the world, then this god that offends their logic, must either be too weak to rid the world of evil, or evil and unjust, or they are not a god at all. The issue with this logic problem is that it is not logical nor a problem. It is a riddle. I will give you an example:

Three people check into a hotel room. The clerk says the bill is $30, so each guest pays $10. Later the clerk realizes the bill should only be $25. To rectify this, he gives the bellhop $5 to return to the guests. On the way to the room, the bellhop realizes that he cannot divide the money equally. As the guests didn't know the total of the revised bill, the bellhop decides to just give each guest $1 and keep $2 as a tip for himself. Each guest got $1 back, so now each guest only paid $9, bringing the total paid to $27. The bellhop has $2. And $27 + $2 = $29 so, if the guests originally handed over $30, what happened to the remaining $1?[65]

If you did not know that this was a riddle you could not know you are being tricked and your confusion would be warranted. The misdirection in this riddle is at the end of the description, where a bunch of unrelated totals are added together, and the listener assumes these numbers should add to thirty. The inquirer leads the listener away from the twenty-five dollars held in the hotel register. If the listener remembers the twenty-five dollars in the till, then they simply add this to the two-dollar bellhop tip and the three-dollar guest refund to get the total of thirty dollars paid by the guests and no money has gone missing.

When people say, "Since evil exists then god is either not good, or not all-powerful," we must recognize that they are NOT giving an answer to the problem of evil injustices – they are posing a riddle. The misdirection in this riddle occurs in the questioner's worldview. This worldview ignores Satan as the easy answer to why evil exists and assumes that if there is a god in charge then he has to follow our timetables and act in ways that we can both see and understand. These assumptions add limits to this god's timing, mercy, and intellect. Only a god who was NOT infinitely wise and powerful would be forced to act in ways that we could both see and understand.

The Epicurean Paradox does not disprove God's existence or justice, because no answers are given. It is a riddle, and, as with all riddles, it is formed to make us look at the problem in the wrong way. Epicurus is looking for a god that he can understand by his own logic and intellect.

I know few people who can understand why their own spouse or children do some of the things they do. Sometimes we do not entirely understand why WE do certain things ourselves. Paul the apostle wrote, "I do not understand what I do; for I don't do what I would like to do, but instead I do what I hate" (Romans 7:15 GNT). How then, can Epicurus demand a god he can comprehend without that god being an imbecile of such small

---

[65] Retrieved on February 23, 2017 from
https://en.wikipedia.org/wiki/Missing_dollar_riddle

intellect that the philosopher himself could explain everything to this god—what they should do, when, and why? Epicurus expects this god to act according to his own timetable.

Realize that if anyone must act according to our timetable, whether god or man, they are our servants. We are in charge, and any power they have is to be used at our discretion. Justice can only be given by the one with the power to enforce it and mercy can only be given by the one who deals justice. Only the one in power can determine when it is right to give justice and when mercy should be given instead. But who should that one be? Should it be you or me? Should it be humanity in general, or a fallen angel like Satan? Only One who loves both the victim and the culprit equally, only One who knows everything, who can gaze into their hearts and minds, can possibly decide between justice and mercy flawlessly. Anyone who cares more for the victim will judge too harshly and anyone who cares more for the culprit will give too much mercy. Only a God who is all-powerful[66] (omnipotent), all-knowing (omniscient),[67] the very incarnation of love,[68] justice and mercy,[69] who is both willing and able to deal with the evil in our world and our lives can determine WHEN the time is right to do so.[70]

The Lord God does not always act in ways we can understand, because He is too smart for us to comprehend how He thinks. A spider has a better chance of understanding the worldwide web of the internet than the combined intellects of mankind has of understanding God. "For my thoughts are not your thoughts, neither are your ways my ways," declares the LORD. "As the heavens are higher than the earth, so are my ways higher than your ways and my thoughts than your thoughts" (Isaiah 55:8,9 NIV). This is one of the reasons God provided so many answers for us in His Holy Bible, so we wouldn't have to rely on our own intellect to understand

---

[66] Then I heard the altar reply, "Yes, Lord God, the All-Powerful, your judgments are true and just!" - Rev 16:7 NIV

[67] . . . For *the* LORD *does* not *see* as man sees; for man looks at the outward appearance, but the LORD looks at the heart. - 1 Samuel 16:7b NKJV

[68] 1 John 4:8, 16

[69] Psalm 103:17, Isaiah 30:18, Jeremiah 9:24

[70] Even Jesus was not told when God, his father, would choose to judge the earth: Matthew 24:35-37, Mark 13:32

Him. Nor does God act according to our timetables.[71]

When speaking of the last days, Peter wrote: "First of all, you must understand that in the last days some people will appear whose lives are controlled by their own lusts. They will make fun of you and will ask, 'He promised to come, didn't he? Where is he? Our ancestors have already died, but everything is still the same as it was since the creation of the world!' . . . But do not forget one thing, my dear friends! There is no difference in the Lord's sight between one day and a thousand years; to him the two are the same. The Lord is not slow to do what he has promised, as some think. Instead, he is patient with YOU, because he does not want anyone to be destroyed, but wants all to turn away from their sins" (2 Peter 3:3-4,8-9 GNT *emphasis added*).

This passage points out that the Lord God of the Bible is not caught by our philosophical riddles, nor will He be rushed to judgement. Instead, God, in His MERCY, patiently waits for everyone who will accept His authority (including His right to be both just and merciful) to stop telling Him what to do and when to do it. We must allow God to be in charge.

When I worked with troubled youth, I discovered many ways people attempt to manipulate others. I soon discovered one of the ways I did this without thinking about it was to ask someone if they could help me with something "right quick." For example, I would say, "Excuse me. Could you hand me that salt right away?" The problem is that it sounds like a polite question, but there is no question that the salt will be handed over. The only question is if it happens quickly enough. The phrasing hides a demand for the salt, and not only that, but also an expectation that it will happen quickly. When we truly ask for help in anything, we are giving up control by putting someone else in charge of whether they will help, how they will help, and when they will do so. If we take any of those decisions out of their hands, then we are not asking. They are not in control of the outcome. We are determining when, and/or how and/or what will be done. We are not asking. We are holding onto control. We are making demands.

I am not the only one who has made this mistake with God. I have heard many people complain that they prayed and prayed, but God did not

---

[71] I wrote a little more about God's power and knowledge in other chapters since they are "easy" answers to some of life's problems.

answer. Really? No, REALLY? You really ASKED God? If so, when did you give up and say God isn't answering? Was it after twenty hours? Days? Weeks? Months? Years? It doesn't matter because YOU chose when to give up. You determined that God was taking too long. Meanwhile, God was probably thinking, "I'm sorry, is there a question in there somewhere? You have made your demands clear as to how and when I must act, but was there something you wanted to ask me for?" Too often, as I find myself waiting for a "prayer" to be answered (sometimes years), I find myself asking God, "What's taking so long?" before I realize that I have been hiding my demands as a prayer. When we ask God to behave in ways, we want Him to, in a timeframe we can find acceptable, we are making the error of Mr. Hume and Epicurus. We are trying to manipulate God. We are putting ourselves in control and demanding "the salt right quick."

What does how we pray have to do with mercy, justice and why life seems so unfair? Life seems unfair when justice is withheld from the righteous (i.e., us) or when mercy is given to those WE deem unworthy. Seldom have I ever needed justice or mercy immediately. Most often I could wait for it. That is why Jesus said, "Happy are those who are merciful to others; God will be merciful to them!" (Matthew 5:7)

When was the last time you saw someone who deserved punishment, but who were so sorry for what they had done and/or who they hurt that your heart melted, and you wanted them to receive mercy instead? It was with little kids, right? Adults are taught to justify their actions. Only the weak ask for mercy—right? We avoid admitting our own fault until it is proven, beyond even our own justifications, that we are at fault.

Remember the story I shared at the beginning of this chapter about when I was in an engineering, graphics and design course? My work was plagiarized, and I was in jeopardy of being flunked out of the class for cheating. Proving my work was my own was not the problem, I had to prove the other guy's work was a copy of my own. I left the office and confronted the other man. He was going to fail the class before he stole my work, so being flunked for stealing was no great punishment for him. He, quite clearly, had no incentive to admit his fault, let alone plead for mercy. I wanted justice . . . and a good dose of vengeance. I knew I could beat the smug look off his face (which I later learned is what he hoped for, because he had access to good, cheap lawyers), but as the thought crossed my mind, another thought pursued it. The second thought was a verse: "Never take revenge, my friends, but instead let God's anger do it. For the scripture says, 'I will take revenge, I will pay back, says the Lord'" (Romans 12:19 GNT). So instead of hurting the thief I chose to walk away and go to God in prayer. I told God the situation and that I was leaving it in His hands to deal with. I had His word on it and I trusted Him to fulfill His promises.

Immediately, I recalled something I had done for fun in my drawings. I went back into the professor's office and asked to see the two sets of blueprints which were submitted. I began flipping through the plagiarized copies, and sure enough, I found the evidence on every page! Since I was planning to use this project in my resume, I had taken the time to hide my name somewhere on every page. On the first page of the plagiarist's work, on the main elevation, was a group of ten shingles in which you could clearly read the name KERRY POCHA. The plagiarist had done such a fine job of tracing my work that he had not noticed my name was on his work! The plagiarist was called in and asked again if he wanted to admit to his crime and get leniency. He knew that the dean did not want to throw me out of school, and he thought I was going to receive whatever punishment he got, so he refused to confess. As such, he was expelled from the course. As a side note: He did receive some mercies from me. He never got hit, and I never pressed charges when I was advised to.

One of the easy answers to life's unfair moments is to recognize that we all need mercy because we have all made mistakes. We have all sinned at various times in our lives.[72] If we want life to start being a little fairer, then we must admit our errors and our need for mercy. We must be willing to give mercy to others and allow God to balance the scales in His own time. The more merciful we are, the more mercy God gives us.

> "God in his mercy has given us this work to do, and so we do not become discouraged. We put aside all secret and shameful deeds; we do not act with deceit, nor do we falsify the word of God. In the full light of truth, we live in God's sight and try to commend ourselves to everyone's good conscience. For if the gospel we preach is hidden, it is hidden only from those who are being lost. They do not believe, because their minds have been kept in the dark by the evil god of this world . . .

---

[72] Romans 3:22-24

For this reason we never become discouraged. Even though our physical being is gradually decaying, yet our spiritual being is renewed day after day. And this small and temporary trouble we suffer will bring us a tremendous and eternal glory, much greater than the trouble. For we fix our attention, not on things that are seen, but on things that are unseen. What can be seen lasts only for a time, but what cannot be seen lasts forever" (2 Corinthians 4:1-4a,16-18 GNT).

If you are not yet a follower of Jesus, you can receive mercy. God offers it freely to all who will admit they've been wrong and want His mercy and forgiveness. Please don't wait or assume that since everyone has sinned, then everyone will get the same treatment.

If you are currently following Jesus, then don't be discouraged when life is unfair. Admit your errors, accept the consequences, pray for those who persecute, insult or use you because, "Blessed are you when people insult you, persecute you and falsely say all kinds of evil against you because of me. Rejoice and be glad, because great is your reward in heaven, for in the same way they persecuted the prophets who were before you" (Matthew 5:11,12 NIV). ". . . and let us run with endurance the race that is set before us, looking unto Jesus, the author and finisher of *our* faith, who for the joy that was set before Him endured the cross, despising the shame, and has sat down at the right hand of the throne of God" (Hebrews 12:1b-2 NKJV).

Remember that the Devil pretends to be God so God will be blamed for the injustices you see, but clearly God knows what He is doing. So, face injustice fearlessly. Be merciful. Be patient. The Author of Justice and Mercy will balance all accounts in His time. You may not see it now, but God has hidden His signature in all His work.

Chapter Seven

The Word of God or "How Does God Speak Today?"

Kerry Pocha

The "Word of God" is an easy answer to many of our hardest problems, but first we must know what the "word of God is. Can we break down the phrase? What does "word" mean, for instance? The English definition of "word" is confusing. It includes a vast array of meanings that give rise to an encompassing understanding, and yet cannot pinpoint any one simple meaning. For instance, I can "give my word," "have a word with someone," "be taken at my word," "look up the word in a dictionary," "put in a good word," "have the last word," "be thought of as a man of few words," "hear a word about a promotion," "word the letter carefully," etc. . . .If I can "give you my word" can you then look up "my word" in a dictionary? A dictionary definition of my written or spoken words may win a court case, but it may not help you to understand what I meant by them.

God's Word is likewise complex. God can "have a word with someone," be "taken at His word," or you could "read His word," God asks, "To whom can I speak and give warning? Who will listen to me? Their ears are closed so they cannot hear. The word of the Lord is offensive to them; they find no pleasure in it" (Jeremiah 6:10 NIV). Simply reading the Bible without allowing God to be heard through it may cause the reader great grief but reading it with a desire to hear from God can give us pleasure, a deeper understanding, and often, the very answer we seek.

In his book, *Surprised by the Voice of God*, Jack Deere relates:

"When the Bible is illumined by the Holy Spirit, its power is incredible. Its light can dispel the darkness of the most convincing Satanic deception. Many since Augustine have been surprised by the power of God's Word. Dorothy is a woman I know who was sinking into suicidal despair. She came to church on Easter Sunday hoping to find an excuse not to take her life. She listened to a sermon on Luke 24, but nothing about it gave her any hope. That night she stood in front of the mirror to say good-bye to a life filled with suffering and despair. As she prepared to commit suicide, a text of scripture rose up in her heart—'Did not the Christ have to suffer these things and then enter his glory?' (Luke 24:26). That was it! First the suffering, then the glory. If she ended her suffering by her own hand, she might miss the glory later. If Christ suffered before he came into his glory, then so would she. She put down the pills and picked up the Bible. The voice of God not only surprised her, but it completely drowned out the demonic voice asking for her life. Such is the power of God's written Word, and such is God's commitment to use it in our lives."[73]

You may have noticed that Mr. Deere refers to the power of God's WRITTEN word, but it was the "voice of God" that surprised the lady he wrote about. This distinction has caused many people to argue over what it means. In ancient Greek (or Roman) societies, a lord could hire a scribe. The lord would then speak aloud (*rhema*) what they wished the scribe to write (*grapho*) in a book, scroll or letter (*gramma*). The lord would then check the document (*gramma*) for errors, omissions and to see if it conveyed the message he intended (*logos*). This makes perfect sense in Greek, but in English all four terms have been translated, at times, as "word." Christians have formed the habit of referring to the entire Bible (*gramma*), a specific verse (*grapho*) in the Bible, what they believe God has said to them (*rhema*), and what God meant (*logos*) as "the Word of God." This can be confusing if you are looking for answers to life's problems in "the Word of God."

Why do Christians interchange these terms instead of inventing new ones or using the old Greek ones. . .? Because we know the author. The voice of God—His *rhema*—is the Holy Spirit. God's children have heard His *rhema* and wrote (*grapho*) to us in the Bible (*gramma*), and by God's *rhema* Christians can find God's *logos*. The apostle John wrote, "Now the *logos* became flesh and took up residence among us" (John 1:14 NET2). He was writing about Jesus. Jesus is the Author and Finisher of our faith.[74] He lived out

---

[73] Surprised by the Voice of God, John S. Deere, (Zondervan Publishing House, 1996), p. 99.

[74] Hebrews 12:2 NKJV

everything His father, God, asked of Him, so Jesus became the living *logos* to a lost and dying world. We saw how God's Word comforted Dorothy and kept her from suicide. She heard the *rhema* of God's Word from the preacher then remembered the *grapho* of a verse, picked up the *gramma* of the Bible and began living the *logos*. I may not understand everything in the Bible as God intended, but I know a guy who does. The author. Jesus is the *logos*, "the living word," and He can explain everything to me by His Holy Spirit.[75] You cannot hear someone talk directly to you until you know them, and you cannot hear from God clearly until you get to know His Son.

In the free daily devotional called *Our Daily Bread*, Tim Gustafson wonders about this "living word of God:" "Why did Jesus come to Earth before the invention of photography and video? Couldn't He have reached more people if everyone could see Him? After all, a picture is worth a thousand words. No. Poet Richard Crashaw states, "The conscious water saw its Master and blushed."[76] In one simple line, Crashaw captures the essence of Jesus' first miracle (John 2:1-11). Creation itself recognizes Jesus as the Creator. No mere carpenter could turn water to wine.

> "Another time, when Christ calmed a storm with the words, 'Quiet! Be still,' His stunned disciples asked, 'Who is this? Even the wind and the waves obey him!' (Mark 4:39, 41). Later, Jesus told the Pharisees that if the crowd did not praise Him, 'the stones will cry out' (Luke 19:40). Even the rocks know who He is."[77]

John tells us, 'The Word became flesh and made his dwelling among us. We have seen His glory.' (John 1:14). Out of that eyewitness experience John also wrote, 'We proclaim to you the one who existed from the beginning, whom we have heard and seen. . .. He is the Word of life' (1 John 1:1 NLT). Like John, we can use our words to introduce others to Jesus, whom wind and water obey.

It seems worthy of note that Jesus spoke a lot about God in his ministry, but unlike the Pharisees and priests at the time, He seldom quoted Scripture verses at his audience. In the Gospel of Mark, Jesus tells a story of a sower,

---

[75] 1 Peter 1:23
[76] Our Daily Bread, March 20, 2016
[77] Ibid.

a field, and seed: "Again, Jesus began to teach by the lake. . . and in his teaching said: 'Listen! A farmer went out to sow his seed. As he was scattering the seed, some fell along the path, and the birds came and ate it up. Some fell on rocky places, where it did not have much soil. It sprang up quickly because the soil was shallow. But when the sun came up, the plants were scorched, and they withered because they had no root. Other seed fell among thorns, which grew up and choked the plants, so that they did not bear grain. Still other seed fell on good soil. It came up, grew and produced a crop, some multiplying thirty, some sixty, some a hundred times.' Then Jesus said, "Whoever has ears to hear, let them hear."

When he was alone, the Twelve and the others around him asked him about the parables. He told them, "The secret of the kingdom of God has been given to you. But to those on the outside everything is said in parables so that, 'they may be ever seeing but never perceiving, and ever hearing but never understanding; otherwise, they might turn and be forgiven!'"

"Then Jesus said to them, 'Don't you understand this parable? How then will you understand any parable? The farmer sows the word. Some people are like seed along the path, where the word is sown. As soon as they hear it, Satan comes and takes away the word that was sown in them. Others, like seed sown on rocky places, hear the word and at once receive it with joy. But since they have no root, they last only a short time. When trouble or persecution comes because of the word, they quickly fall away. Still others, like seed sown among thorns, hear the word; but the worries of this life, the deceitfulness of wealth and the desires for other things come in and choke the word, making it unfruitful. Others, like seed sown on good soil, hear the word, accept it, and produce a crop—some thirty, some sixty, some a hundred times what was sown'" (Mark 4:1a, 2b – 20 NIV).

Notice how Jesus keeps saying that people "hear the word" and then respond in different ways? The sower and the seed never change, but the soil of the hearer does. God's Spirit and His word never change, but our hearts can, and do.

I have noticed, in my forty-plus years of following Jesus' teachings, that when someone hears from Jesus, whether through His Bible, a preacher, friend, co-worker, or even a majestic sunset, they are changed. Even if they reject what He has said, they are changed. They either turn to listen to what

God is saying, or they turn and flee from His words. Either way, they will not remain where they are. Undoubtedly, this is why God tells us in Isaiah 55:11: "…so is my word that goes out from my mouth: It will not return to me empty, but will accomplish what I desire and achieve the purpose for which I sent it."

What is the purpose of God's Word? To transform the very earth. Seed can convert dead soil into a living thing. What do you think God's Word could do to your life if you let it? What is God asking you to do? Be transformed into His likeness and go change the world around you.

Gardeners will spend many hours cultivating the soil prior to planting. They remove rocks, soften the soil by turning it, and add nutrients to enrich it. After planting, they return regularly to water their garden and pull unwanted weeds. Our hearts and lives require no less attention.

The world instructs us to harden ourselves to the hardships around us, but God tells us to soften our hearts and be compassionate.[78] The mature follower of Jesus will receive hardships, and persecutions as a gardener receives a sack of manure. What others would throw away and ignore, the gardener takes with joyful gratitude to enrich a crop that may not yet even be planted. The gardener looks beyond what is seen and trusts in the power of the seed to draw what it needs to make something good from what others thought to be nasty or harmful.[79]

The soft soul is ready to receive God's word and allows it to be thrust deep into their heart. God's Holy Spirit is welcomed as rain upon their crops, and any thought or seed not from God is recognized as an invasive weed in their life, only there to steal life from the fruit they are trying to grow.

Easy answers to many of life's problems come from God's Word—His Living Word. Have you prepared your heart to serve God or are you hardening your heart to resist His planting? Love, joy, peace, forbearance, kindness, goodness, faithfulness, gentleness, and self-control are the fruits God offers to grow in those who seek Him,[80] "but the worries of this life, the deceitfulness of wealth and the desires for other things come in and choke the word, making it unfruitful" (Mark 4:19 NIV). Where are you

---

[78] Ephesians 4:32, Colossians 3:12, 1 Peter 3:8
[79] Genesis 50:20 NKJV
[80] Galatians 5:22,23a

buying your seed? How often do you invite Him in to sow His seed? How often do you allow the enemy to sow bad seed?

I am going to end with a short story from my prayer journal about how God used three words and a strange dream to transform the sorrows of my life into a hopeful attitude:

"I woke up this morning sad and wanted to talk to God about how discouraged I was feeling. I had left my journal at church, so I grabbed an old one to see if it had a blank page or two left. On the back cover I had written E Vitium Sanctus. I remembered why. I had a dream once but cannot find the notes I wrote about it. I recall the dream something like this:

"A war was raging around me. Flame and explosions. Enemy gunfire and I was in a trench. In front of me was a no-man's-land, filled with craters, mud, and slick with blood. Nothing survived there.

"I held my head low and looked at the dirt bank in front of me, like the edge of a grave. I could feel my heart pound and the ground shake around me. I thought 'Lord help', then raised my head and said, 'On my command!' Trying to ready myself for the charge, I wondered if I would be alone. So, I looked from one side to the other and as far as I could see there were angels, crammed into the trench, crouched and ready to pounce. They were larger than Arctic grizzly bears, staring forward with an eager anticipation. Waiting . . . waiting . . . Waiting on what—me? I could barely reach the top of the trench and the Angel next to me could barely fit into the trench. I immediately thought 'On my command? Who am I to command you?' The Angel turned his head and looked respectfully down at me and in a slow deliberate growl said, "E . . . VITIUM . . . SANCTUS," then turned back and grabbed the top of the trench.

As I turned to the enemy, jumped out of the trench, and ran, I screamed "CHARGE!" with a ferocity that scared even me. I knew with absolute certainty that this victory was already won.

"I immediately awoke and wondered what those words the Angel said to me meant. Why was I so invigorated from three words in a language I did not understand? I thought it sounded like Latin, so I went to my computer to get a translation and discovered the Angel in my dream had told me I was worthy of leading him into battle because I was "called out of sin and into Holy devotion to God."

E(Out of / from) **VITIUM**(defect / vice / sin) into **SANCTUS**(Holy, sacred, a saint)[81]

I am given the authority to call on God`s angel armies, because of who I am. I have gone "from being a sinner to a saint." I have been pulled from the miry clay[82] of my sin and reborn as a holy child of God.[83] Out of my selfish vices, I have become devoted to God. The word of God has told me so.

So, how does God speak to the world today? If you are a Christian, the easy answer is—you. Christian means "little Christ," and whether you are only a little like Christ or a lot, you are God's Living Word to a lost and dying world—a "little Christ." God's very Spirit lives within you,[84] and by that Spirit He speaks to the world. And what would God's Spirit like to tell the world?

It is the word of faith that welcomes God to go to work and set things right for us. This is the core of our preaching. Say the welcoming word to God, "Jesus is my Master," embracing, body and soul, God's work of doing in us what he did in raising Jesus from the dead. That's it. You're not "doing" anything; you're simply calling out to God, trusting Him to do it for you. That's salvation. With your whole being you embrace God setting things right, and then you say it, right out loud: "God has set everything right between Him and me!"

Scripture reassures us, "No one who trusts God like this—heart and soul— will ever regret it." It's exactly the same no matter what a person's religious background may be: the same God for all of us, acting the same incredibly generous way to everyone who calls out for help. "Everyone who calls, 'Help, God!' gets help" (Romans 10:8b-13 The Message).

Could you hear God's word speak to you today? Only if you listen.

---

[81] Retrieved on October 26, 2019 from https://www.math.ubc.ca/~cass/frivs/latin/latin-dict-full.html#L

[82] Psalm 40:2 NKJV

[83] John 1:2

[84] Acts 1:5,8; 2:17,33,38; Romans 8:9,11,15, 15:30; 1 Corinthians 2:13, 3:16; Galatians 3:3; Ephesians 1:3, 3:16, 5:18, 6:18; 2 Thessalonians 2:13; 1 Peter 4:14; 1 John 2:27, 4:4; Jude 1:19

Chapter Eight

The Knowledge of God or "How Can I Follow an Invisible God?"

Kerry Pocha

T he Knowledge of God can be an easy answer in our times of trouble . . . or it can be useless. It can be a simple solution, or an additional complication in our struggles. Why? Because its not just what you know, its WHO you know. J. I. Packer wrote an entire book about the knowledge of God, as John previously mentioned. In it, Packer stated, "Once you become aware that the main business that you are here for is to know God, most of life's problems fall into place of their own accord." [85] Easy. I have found, through much trial and error, that Mr. Packer was correct. If, for instance, you need a loan, would you rather know where a bank is, know what its loan policies are, or know the owner personally? Knowing the owner means that they can take you to the bank, help you fill out the forms properly, or even ignore them and give you some cash out of their personal account. That is why it has been said, "Bible study without Bible experience is pointless. Knowing Psalm 23 is different from knowing the shepherd."[86]

There are two things which the author of Hebrews (that's a book in the Bible I'm referring to not just someone who writes in Hebrew, so if you have not read the book lately, do so now; it takes about an hour and it is more important than reading this book so we can wait . . .)

OK, back to the author of Hebrews. The apostle Paul says there are a couple of things we must first know about God before we can approach Him: 1) the one who comes to God must know that He is, and 2) that He

---

[85] Retrieved from https://www.goodreads.com/quotes/327235-once-you-become-aware-that-the-main-business-that-you

[86] Retrieved fromhttps://www.goodreads.com/quotes/tag/knowing-god – quote of Kingsley Opuwari Manuel

rewards those who diligently seek Him.[87] In other words, we must first know that He is God and that He is good.

We must first KNOW that God exists. What is knowledge, but a firm belief in what we have already learned, and what is faith but a willingness to act on that belief. The difference between belief and faith is the difference between knowledge and trust, awareness and relationship, hypocrisy, and power. Many people say they believe in the God of Creation but act every day as if the artist does not exist and the painting evolved from a stray bit of canvas blowing in the wind. Knowing that there is a god in heaven is not the same as knowing THE God in heaven. That is why the Bible states: "You believe that there is one God. Good! Even the demons believe that— and shudder" (James 2:19 NIV). We must first know God exists, then trust that He rewards those who diligently seek Him. All relationships begin with an awareness that the other person exists, but just knowing that your favourite actor exists does not mean that you have a relationship with them. Many people know ABOUT God. They can be very friendly, and charismatic as they help you understand Him better. They are often sought out as leaders of churches or gurus of some kind or other, but they have no relationship with God—the Father. Jesus put it this way: "Not all who sound religious are really godly people. They may refer to me as 'Lord,' but still won't get to heaven. For the decisive question is whether they obey my Father in heaven. At the Judgment many will tell me, 'Lord, Lord, we told others about you and used your name to cast out demons and to do many other great miracles.' But I will reply, 'You have never been mine. Go away, for your deeds are evil'" (Matthew 7:21-23 TLB).

I notice a couple of important things in this passage: one is that there is power in the name of Jesus, even if you don't know Him, and the other is that knowing *about* Jesus is NOT the same thing as knowing Jesus.

Nicky Gumbel, an English Anglican priest, in his introduction to "Alpha," his Christianity course, uses a metaphor to describe the difference between knowing God and knowing about Him:

". . . you can't prove Christianity scientifically. Science is obviously quite important, but science answers a different set of questions. Science answers the questions, when, and how this world came into being, but

---

[87] Hebrews 11:6

cannot answer the question who, and why it came into being.

Suppose I had a cake here, which I have made, and I give it to a scientist. The scientist will be able to answer the question: 'how it was made?' they may even be able to tell you when it was made, but only I can tell you who made it and why I made it. Only the creator of the cake can do that."[88]

Many people travel the globe looking for ways to know who made them and why but miss the easy answers. God made us and He made us to know and love Him. God is infinite and, thus, unknowable by any means we have in or of ourselves, yet He allows Himself to be known by those who love Him. In fact, He explains himself to us in the simplest manner so that anyone who wants to know how to have a good, uncomplicated life can. When asked, by a religious leader the best way to impress God (i.e., "what is the greatest commandment?"[89]), Jesus gave him the easy answer: "Love God, love People." It's that easy to know God. This is the heart of what it takes to follow Jesus. So simple. So hard. Jesus said, "I am the way, the truth, and the life. No one comes to the Father except through Me," (John 14:6 NKJV); and, "Take my yoke upon you and learn from me, for I am gentle and humble in heart, and you will find rest for your souls. For my yoke is easy and my burden is light," (Matthew 11:29-30 NIV). Love God, love people, and God's own Son promises to help when we do these two things. He is "yoked" together with us in this "burden."

Now, have you ever wanted to know what God's will is for you in life? I have lost my appetite over this in the past and refused to eat until I knew God's will for me. Though the answer we get may be slightly more specific, the gist is always the same: Love God and love people. It is what God does. It is what Jesus lived out. It is what the Apostles, and every sincere Christian tries to do. If we do these things, in even the tiniest of ways, we can move mountains.[90]

You have now heard the truth and it is in your head as knowledge, but do you believe it? Are you willing to trust it enough to change your life, and

---

[88] Retrieved from https://www.youtube.com/watch?v=HtTnSMNtE44 time stamp: 4:14 – 4:55
[89] Matthew 22:34-40, Luke 10:25-28
[90] Matthew 17:20, 21:21, Luke 17:6, Mark 11:23

start making decisions based on that knowledge? In other words, do you genuinely believe what you believe?

We all need to know what we truly "believe." It is our worldview. It is how we choose to explain what happens in the world and why. The author of Hebrews, however, says that "faith is to be sure of the things we hope for, to be certain of the things we cannot see" (Hebrews 11:1 GNT). This is not a blind, foolish faith in some ridiculous invention of our minds. Our "faith" is the actions we choose based on our beliefs. My favourite old dictionary says, "Faith is a union of belief and trust. Faith is often personal; belief may be quite impersonal, but as soon as belief is strong enough to be followed by definite action, the belief becomes faith."[91] You see, faith is not simply, as is commonly thought today, a belief in something we cannot prove. Faith includes the actions that show what we honestly believe.

The faith spoken of in Hebrews is like the faith most people have in the applied sciences. No one gets onto a plane without having confidence in the things they hope for. Our simple hope is that the plane will take-off and land safely. This confidence comes, not only, from the things we can see, like the pilot, and plane, but more so, from things we cannot see, like gravity, aeronautics, and the air itself. If we were truly honest with ourselves, we would have to admit that we are more confident in the unseen than the seen. We are, for instance, more confident in the existence of gravity and air than the pilot's ability or the plane itself. Yet we trust the pilot to get us to our destination safely. We are certain of the things we cannot see, and less sure of the things we hope for; we have faith every time we choose to get onto a plane, car, bicycle or even sit upon a chair. First, we choose to trust the maker of the chair. Then we try the chair. This experience gives us confidence to trust and try other chairs. Eventually we learn to trust the unseen manufacturers of bicycles, then cars, and finally planes.

Likewise, Christians are given opportunities to grow their trust in God. God gives us things of little worth, like money, to help us learn how to be faithful and trustworthy. Only then will He give us the greater gifts. Jesus said, "So if you have not been trustworthy in handling worldly wealth, who will trust you with true riches? . . . What people value highly is detestable in

---

[91] faith, "Funk and Wagnalls New Practical Standard Dictionary," vol. 1, New York: Funk and Wagnalls Company, 1951.

God's sight" (Luke 16:10,15b NIV). To know God is to know what is important to Him.

The people who are the closest to God are said to walk with Him. That is because, being close to God and knowing Him well are actions. No one should ever preach: "Sit on your butt, relax and do nothing and God will come find you to love and snuggle you," because He will not do so. God loves you and will chase after you relentlessly until you turn away from your selfishness and toward Him. Then He expects you to stop running away and chase after Him as relentlessly as He chased after you. If you have ever been in love with someone you should know that it only stops being fun when you stop chasing one another. If you ever start chasing wealth, power, prestige, happiness, or anything else outside your marriage, other than God, your marriage will start to fall apart. It is the same way with God. Jesus pointed out that, "No one can serve two masters. Either you will hate the one and love the other, or you will be devoted to the one and despise the other" (Luke 16:13a NIV).

So, knowing God is like walking with Him, but more like being married to Him. It is a life-long pursuit of getting to know and trust Him more and more every day. If we continue to do so each day, eventually we will learn not only to trust Him to bear the weight of our troubles, like a chair, but also to lift us up beyond the day-to-day cares and sins that so easily drag our hearts down. Isaiah the prophet wrote: "But those who trust in the LORD will find new strength. They will soar high on wings like eagles. They will run and not grow weary. They will walk and not faint" (Isaiah 40:31 NLT).

Yes, as we learn to not just get information about God, like a seedy private detective looking for incriminating evidence they can use to manipulate someone, and instead learn to commit ourselves to loving and understanding the One who was willing to die for us, we can begin to receive the "true riches" Jesus spoke about. Many of these riches are spoken of in other chapters of this book. Riches like love, joy, peace, and hope are attained when our innermost heart and desires, our spirit, is in harmony with God's desires, His Holy Spirit. In other words, God's love, joy, peace, hope etc... can only be received when we want to know how to please Him more than we want to receive His gifts. Then God gives us both, and we can echo the great evangelist, missionary, and martyr, Jim Elliot, as he wrote in his journal: "I walked out to the hill just now. It is exalting, delicious. To stand embraced by the shadows of a friendly tree with the wind tugging at your coattail and the heavens hailing your heart, to gaze and glory and to give oneself again to God, what more could a man ask? Oh, the fullness, pleasure, sheer excitement of knowing God on earth. I care not if I never raise my voice again for Him, if only I may love Him, please Him. Perhaps, in mercy, He shall give me a host of children that I may lead through the vast star fields to explore His delicacies whose fingers' ends set them to burning. But if not, if only I may see Him, smell His garments, and smile into my Lover's eyes, ah, then, not stars, nor children, shall matter—only Himself."[92]

Do you want to love someone like that? Then get to know the Source of True Love, Jesus, personally and intimately. The apostle Peter put it this way: "Everything that goes into a life of pleasing God has been miraculously given to us by getting to know, personally and intimately, the One who invited us to God. The best invitation we ever received! We were also given terrific promises to pass on to you—your tickets to participation in the life of God after you turned your back on a world corrupted by lust. So, don't lose a minute in building on what you've been given, complementing your basic faith with good character, spiritual understanding, alert discipline, passionate patience, reverent wonder, warm friendliness, and generous love, each dimension fitting into and developing the others. With these qualities active and growing in your lives, no grass will grow under your feet, no day will pass without its reward as you mature in your experience of our Master Jesus. Without these qualities you can't see what's right before you, oblivious that your old sinful life has been wiped off the books. So, friends, confirm God's invitation to you, his choice of you. Don't put it off; do it now. Do this, and you'll have your life on a firm footing, the streets paved and the way wide open into the eternal kingdom of our Master and Savior, Jesus Christ" (2 Peter 1:3-11 The Message).

John and I cannot agree more... don't just learn about Jesus and His Father, God. Accept His invitation to know Him, personally and intimately. "Don't put it off; do it now."

The easy answer to the question, "How can I follow an invisible God?" is to get to know Him on a personal level. Choose to believe what He tells

---

[92] Retrieved from https://www.goodreads.com/quotes/8896449-i-walked-out-to-the-hill-just-now-it-is

you through His word.[93] Then, to your belief—add trust. As you walk out your growing faith, you will find it becomes easier and easier to trust God in every area of your life. With each "baby step" the legs of your faith will grow stronger, until you find yourself running and taking leaps of faith, until one day you leap so high that He catches you, and the pull of this earth is overcome by your trust in Him. Then you will find yourself rising, as if on eagles' wings.

---

[93] Re-read the previous chapter on the 'Word of God' to get a better understanding of how God speaks to us.

Chapter Nine

The Power of God or "What do I do if I've lost my Purpose in Life?"

Kerry Pocha

In 2011, a powerful earthquake hit Japan. "It was the most powerful earthquake ever recorded to have hit Japan, and the fifth most powerful earthquake in the world since modern record-keeping began in 1900. The earthquake triggered powerful tsunami waves that reached heights of up to 40.5 metres (133 feet) in Miyako in Tōhoku's Iwate Prefecture, and which, in the Sendai area, travelled up to 10 kilometres (6 miles) inland. The earthquake moved Honshu (the main island of Japan) 2.4 metres (8 feet) east and shifted the Earth on its axis by estimates of between 10 cm (4 inches) and 25 centimetres (10 in)."[94] It's hard to imagine anything more powerful than this catastrophic event but the truth is that there are powerful things that happen frequently in a negative way.

There is no need to detail the power of sickness, hate, and other destructive forces, but the easy answer to all those impacts is the power of God. Later we will see that God is much greater than all the storms of life. The power of God is not like a car engine that sits in a garage collecting dust. The power of God is active and can be active for your situation. But how? Is God's power available to anyone? Is God a force that we can plug into at will, or is He a capricious child who withholds all His toys just to show His power over us? Neither! God is not a power source to be utilized at our whim, or by rituals, cleansings, spells, or incantations, nor is His power given at random, without rhyme or reason. There are reasons for every miracle He does, and we can observe the rhyme scheme of how and why we see such things throughout Scripture.

The apostle Paul said to the believers in Corinth that he "will find out not only how these arrogant people are talking, but what power they have. For

---

[94] Retrieved June 2, 2016 from http://en.wikipedia.org/wiki/Japan_tsunami

the kingdom of God is not a matter of talk but of power" (1 Cor. 4:19,20). In other words, Paul knew that the true sign that God is working in your life is not how holy or pious what you are doing and saying is, but rather if the power of God is being manifest through you. "God did extraordinary miracles through Paul, so that even handkerchiefs and aprons that had touched him were taken to those who were ill, and their illnesses were cured and the evil spirits left them" (Acts 19:11,12). The writer of Acts points out that God did extraordinary miracles through Paul. If the miracles done through Paul were extraordinary, then God apparently does other miracles that are commonplace or ordinary. Are you seeing the power of God in your life? Start by looking for the "ordinary" miracles God does and thank Him for those. When we are grateful for the *what* God is doing in our lives, we begin to see God pour out blessings in unexpected ways. This takes practice, but it is worth it.

Not everything we go through is going to be easily recognized as good. To learn right from wrong, a child must experience the pain of their wrong choices. If a parent protects their child from consequences, that child, like a lovely, sweet, wax coated apple, will rot from the inside. Jesus taught us to see God's blessings in the most unexpected places when He gave the Roman-oppressed nation of Israel His sermon on the mount. In the sermon, He gave them the "beatitudes." These beautiful attitudes were followed by blessings from God. I like how Eugene Peterson paraphrases these blessings for our modern ears: "You're blessed when you're at the end of your rope. With less of you there is more of God and his rule. You're blessed when you feel you've lost what is most dear to you. Only then can you be embraced by the One most dear to you. You're blessed when you're content with just who you are—no more, no less. That's the moment you find yourselves proud owners of everything that can't be bought. You're blessed when you've worked up a good appetite for God. He's food and drink in the best meal you'll ever eat. You're blessed when you care. At the moment of being 'care-full,' you find yourselves cared for. You're blessed when you get your inside world—your mind and heart—put right. Then you can see God in the outside world. You're blessed when you can show people how to cooperate instead of competing or fight. That's when you discover who you really are, and your place in God's family. You're blessed when your commitment to God provokes persecution. The persecution drives you even deeper into God's kingdom. Not only that—count yourselves blessed every time people put you down or throw you out or speak lies about you to discredit me. What it means is that the truth is too close for comfort and they are uncomfortable. You can be glad when that happens—give a cheer, even! —for though they don't like it, *I* do! And all heaven applauds. And know that you are in good company. My prophets and witnesses have always gotten into this kind of trouble. (Matthew 5:3-12 MSG)

"I don't know about you, but I do not feel blessed when I am 'at the end of my rope' or have 'lost what is most dear to me'! I have noticed, however, that those are the times I find myself able to squeeze in tighter to God than I have ever done so before. Afterwards, I have found greater strength to face the world and its ruler, Satan. Afterwards, I can face imminent trials with a knowledge that when I am doing what I think God wants me to do, He is pleased to be with me through it, and when God is with me even death is afraid to see me coming!

"Does that sound boastful? If it does, I will boast some more, because I am not boasting in myself. I am boasting in the power of my Lord and saviour Jesus Christ![95] For when he died on the cross God treated Jesus like he had lived my sinful life, so that I could be treated as if I had lived his. When Jesus died, he was buried, but before his body could be prepared, God raised his son from the dead![96] Death could not hold him."[97]

Sin is the handle death uses to drag people into Hell, but there was no sin handle on Jesus. In fact, it was as if the Holy Spirit of God had slathered Him in grease. Jesus walked free and now we can give up our old, sin-filled lives and exchange them for living a sin-free, death-free life. Are you afraid of death, or is death afraid of you? If you are afraid of losing your life, what is most dear to you, you will never be able to truly live a life filled with God's power. God wants to fill your life with His power, but how can He if it is already filled with what you want. Your desires will always displace God's desires. You cannot fill a cup with both clean water and dirt. You will only end up with muck. So, clean your cup of ingratitude and open your eyes to the provision God has already given you.

---

[95] 1 Corinthians 1:31, 2 Corinthians 10:17, 12:19

[96] 1 Corinthians 15:3-8

[97] Matthew 28:5-7, Acts 2:32, Romans 4:25-5:19

In 2 Kings 4:1-7 (GNT) the Bible tells us of a woman in deep trouble: "The widow of a member of a group of prophets went to Elisha and said, 'Sir, my husband has died! As you know, he was a God-fearing man, but now a man he owed money to has come to take away my two sons as slaves in payment for my husband's debt.' 'What shall I do for you?' he asked. 'Tell me, what do you have at home?' 'Nothing at all, except a small jar of olive oil,' she answered. 'Go to your neighbors and borrow as many empty jars as you can,' Elisha told her. 'Then you and your sons go into the house, close the door, and start pouring oil into the jars. Set each one aside as soon as it is full.' So, the woman went into her house with her sons, closed the door, took the small jar of olive oil, and poured oil into the jars as her sons brought them to her. When they had filled all the jars, she asked if there were any more. 'That was the last one,' one of her sons answered. And the olive oil stopped flowing. She went back to Elisha, the prophet, who said to her, 'Sell the olive oil and pay all your debts, and there will be enough money left over for you and your sons to live on.'"

To see the miracle, the widow had to believe that God, NOT ELISHA, would provide for her. She could then go to the man of God knowing that God's power was available to her. Next, the widow had to see that she had some oil before the miracle could happen. If she would have pouted and simply whined at Elisha that she had "nothing," then nothing is what she would have received, but she began with a small realization of gratitude by admitting that she had "a small jar of olive oil." Now she was put in a position where she had to do something herself. Obedience was required. If she didn't gather jars, then she would have nothing to receive the blessing in. She was told, "Don't ask for just a few." This tested her faith.

How big is the blessing God has for you? God has an ocean of powerful blessing to bestow on the ones who love and obey Him, but often we get lazy or feel foolish gathering pots when we have no oil, so we end up bringing a thimble to receive our miracle. If this has been you, then tell God you are sorry for your lack of belief and ask Him to "help you in your unbelief."[98] Your miracle may be waiting on your humility.

When I first read 2 Timothy 3 and its warning against poor behaviour in perilous times, I was only about nine years old, and I was confident I was

---

[98] Mark 9:23-24

doing well. I didn't love myself. I didn't even really like myself much. I had no money to love, and nothing to boast about, so I had no danger of getting conceited. I only had to be sure to try and obey my parents and be grateful for the roof over my head, but by the time I was in my late twenties, I was looking to settle down and get married. I was proud of what I had accomplished. I had big dreams and solid plans to get them. I had a decent income and knew how to relax on my time off. I worked hard and played hard. Employers and co-workers thought of me as a good, if not godly, man and I could explain to any would-be clients, employees, or employers how I could use my massive skill set for their benefit.

I knew how to accomplish almost anything I set my mind to. I attended church regularly and had God as a friend. What more could I want? I was truly blessed. Right? I did not know that I had a form of godliness but none of HIS power in my life. All the power I had was mine, and mine to toy with. I loved investing my income and watch as my investments grew steadily. I had become a lover of money. It gave me the power to enjoy life and not worry about how things got done. If I wanted something, I bought it. Were my new shoes made by child labourers? I didn't know, or care. My love of God and His goodness was growing cold. God saw what I could not. I needed more than I had to get through the "terrible times" that were coming. I needed God's power.

It wasn't until my wife left me and took our new-born with her that I learned how to come to God "in-sack-cloth-and-ashes," so to speak. I had lost my wife, child, home, career, business, dreams, and I thought -- God. I realized all these hopes and dreams were the purposes I had given myself. Without those hopes and dreams I had no purpose in life. I was at the end of my rope and ready to die. Only a couple of things stayed my hand from taking my own life. My baby girl, and the knowledge that God had given me this life. Since He gave me this life, I knew it wasn't mine to take, it was up to God to determine when I would die. Logically, I could blame Him, then, for allowing all the misery I was living through. So, I did. But I was wrong.

God wasn't to blame. He tried to warn me that I could not pursue both Him and money. We could not both be in control of my life. Either I lived a life I could brag about, OR I choose to live a life God would brag about. I could dream up what I did with my life, OR I could live God's purpose-filled dream for me. Either my purpose in life was based on things that could be taken away, like money, health, friendships, or family, OR my true purpose was something greater, something that could never be taken away, something eternal. I knew then that I would never base my hopes on anything I could lose again. My hopes would only ever be based on the eternal saving gift of Jesus Christ's death and resurrection. The reward which God promised to all who believe in his son.[99]

You're cheating on God. If all you want is your own way, flirting with the world every chance you get, you end up enemies of God and his way. And do you suppose God doesn't care? The proverb has it that 'he's a fiercely jealous lover.' And what he gives in love is far better than anything else you'll find. It's common knowledge that "God goes against the wilfully proud; God gives grace to the willing humble."

"So let God work his will in you. Yell a loud no to the Devil and watch him make himself scarce. Say a quiet yes to God and he'll be there in no time. Quit dabbling in sin. Purify your inner life. Quit playing the field. Hit bottom, and cry your eyes out. The fun and games are over. Get serious, really serious. Get down on your knees before the Master; it's the only way you'll get on your feet" (James 4:4-10 MSG).

Are you looking for an easy answer because your dreams are crumbling around you? Then welcome to the club! It is hard but try to remember that "You're blessed when you're at the end of your rope. With less of you there is more of God and his rule." I discovered that Rick Warren was right in his book, *A Purpose Driven Life*, when he said, "You never know God is all you need until God is all you have."[100] He then went on to say, "If not to God, you will surrender to the opinions or expectations of others, to money, to resentment, to fear, or to your own pride, lusts, or ego. You were designed to worship God and if you fail to worship Him, you will create other things (idols) to give your life to. You are free to choose, what you surrender to but you are not free from the consequence of that choice."[101]

So, what are you surrendered to? Before God can put any power into your

---

[99] Romans 1:16, 2 Corinthians 6:2, 2 Corinthians 7:10, Titus 2:11, Hebrews 9:28, 1 Peter 1:5, 9, Revelation 7:10, 12:10

[100] Retrieved from https://quotefancy.com/quote/899581/Rick-Warren-You-never-know-God-is-all-you-need-until-God-is-all-you-have

[101] Warren, R. (2007). Chapter 10 -The Heart of Worship. In *The purpose driven life: What on earth am I here for, Rick Warren* (p. 55). Grand Rapids, Michigan: Zondervan.

life you have to give the power you wield in your life to Him—you must surrender. You can only get power from one place at a time.

You may have noticed that I have not given anything specific that must be done to see God's power in your life. Instead, like Jesus, I have shown how your attitude can stop, or limit, God's power in your life. It is God's choice to respect your choices. He chooses to limit His power in the lives of those who put limits on Him.

I have defined faith before as, "how we act on what we believe." As Tim Allen was told in the movie *The Santa Clause,* © "Seeing isn't believing. Believing is seeing." There are many things we cannot see that we act upon every day. You cannot see gravity, but you refuse to jump off tall buildings without some way to save you from its pull. Love, pain, and thought also are as invisible and intangible as God, yet we mould our lives daily around our beliefs that they exist. When I choose to believe in the invisible, then I can choose to interact with it by faith. With a firm belief in gravity and air, the Wright Brothers invented a motorized aircraft, and twenty-four years later, Charles Lindbergh flew solo across the Atlantic Ocean. Today we have international air travel. What could God do with you and a firm belief in Jesus and the power of His Holy Spirit?

The Christian band **Newsong** wrote:

I hear you say that it all sounds crazy
It's a good story but it can't be true
How could a man who was dead and buried
Mean a thing to me and you?

Here we are two thousand years later
And still the choice is just the same
You can say that you don't believe it
But it doesn't change a thing . . .

I can take you to the hill
Where they hung Him on a cross
I can take to the empty tomb
I can tell you He's alive
'Cause He lives in me
But the rest is up to you!

You can close your eyes
You can say it's a lie
You can stick your head in the sand

You can turn away, even try to explain
He was just another man
When they nailed Him to the cross by His hands and feet
And the put Him in the ground
Three days later everybody found out that you can't
No you can't keep a good man down! . . .[102]

What is your purpose in life? Where are you getting the strength and power to complete that purpose? Are your hopes and dreams dying? Relationships fading? Has your purpose for living been lost? Then you had them based on something that could be taken away.

If you, like I once had, have lost your reason(s) to live, then the easy answer is to stop looking for temporary things to fulfill your eternal purpose. There is a God in Heaven, and He has the power to bring the dead to life! As Pastor Rick Warren said, "You were designed to worship God." So, worship God with everything you have, and you will never lose your reason to live again. We are eternal beings; we must have eternal purposes.

---

[102] Song lyrics retrieved from
https://www.lyrics.com/lyric/4309696/Can%27t+Keep+a+Good+Man+Down, "You can't keep a good man down", from the Newsong Album "KLTY Presents: Celebrate Freedom Live", 2000, Lyrics © Sony/ATV Music Publishing LLC, THE BICYCLE MUSIC COMPANY, CAPITOL CHRISTIAN MUSIC GROUP

Chapter Ten

The Presence of God or "Where is God When I Hurt?"

John W. Telman

To many people, the presence of God is not an easy answer, nor is it desired. Their perception of God is skewed and causes them to resist the presence of God, even if they acknowledge His existence. Kerry touched on this in a previous chapter when he showed us that, to some, the company of God is not wanted but is to be resisted.

In the apocalyptic book of the Revelation, we read that someday, people will cry out "to the mountains and to the rocks, 'Fall on us and hide us from the presence of Him who sits on the throne, and from the wrath of the Lamb; for the great day of their wrath has come, and who is able to stand?'" (Revelation 6:16, 17). The presence of God will be so horrible for those who have rejected Him repeatedly, but for the person who places their trust in God, His presence is an easy answer.

Dr. George Westlake wrote, "God has not promised us a bed of roses on which to stroll to heaven. He has promised difficulty. But along with difficulty, He has promised to be there to sustain us and see us through."[103] Westlake also adds a powerful passage of scripture which encourages everyone who is suffering.

> "Fear not: for I have redeemed thee, I have called thee by thy name; thou art mine. When thou passest through the waters, I will be with thee; and through the rivers, they shall not overflow thee; when thou walkest through the fire, thou shalt not be burned; neither shall the flame kindle upon thee" (Isaiah 43:1-2 KJV).

Three friends of the prophet Daniel understood this by experience.

---

[103] "The Most Often Asked Questions on Sunday Night Alive", George Westlake, 1997, p. 241-242

Hananiah, Mishael and Azariah[104] were forced to worship a statue of the King of Babylon. Under threat of death, they would not. They replied to the King by saying, "Our God whom we serve is able to deliver us from the furnace of blazing fire; and He will deliver us out of your hand, O King. But even if He does not, let it be known to you, O King, that we are not going to serve your gods or worship the golden image that you have set up" (Daniel 3:17, 18). These young men trusted that God would be with them even though the problem was life threatening. God did not disappoint. They were sentenced and thrown into a furnace so hot that the executioners were killed by the flames (Daniel 3:22), but the three young men were spared. The flame did not kindle upon them and the bonus was that the Son of God was right there with them. The very King who sentenced them witnessed this miracle of the presence of God.

"When Jesus returned to Capernaum, a Roman officer came and pleaded with him, 'Lord, my young servant lies in bed, paralyzed and in terrible pain.' Jesus said, 'I will come and heal him.' But the officer said, 'Lord, I am not worthy to have you come into my home. Just say the word from where you are, and my servant will be healed. I know this because I am under the authority of my superior officers, and I have authority over my soldiers. I only need to say, "Go," and they go, or "Come," and they come. And if I say to my slaves, "Do this," they do it.' When Jesus heard this, he was amazed. Turning to those who were following him, he said, 'I tell you the truth, I haven't seen faith like this in all Israel!'" (Matthew 8:5-10). In this passage of scripture, we learn wonderful truths about Jesus Christ.

Jesus was willing to enter the home of a Roman soldier who was the sworn enemy of the Jews.

The Jews wanted their oppressor out of their country, and they were waiting for the Messiah to be the ultimate military leader to free them. After all, if a slave were ever sick, most Romans would just kill them to free themselves from the expense and responsibility of caring for the health of the slave, but Jesus was willing to come and heal the slave. He was willing to enter the home of the Roman oppressor.

What a wonderful picture. Jesus, the holy one of God will dare to come to

---

[104] Most commonly known by the pagan names given them of Shadrach, Meshach and Abed-nego

where sinners dwell. The truth is, even though we may try to hide our sins from our families or friends, God is aware of them. The good news is that Jesus was going to the Roman soldier's home, not to condemn but to heal. Jesus cares about what concerns us, including those who are perceived to be the enemy. Even though He is the Holy One of God, Jesus desires to come and heal those who are sick in body and spirit.

We need Jesus! We need His healing! We need Him to make a house call! He is one doctor who still makes house calls! Even to the spiritually bankrupt, He comes, but in this scripture passage, Jesus was the healer of the physically sick. He is both the spiritual healer and the physical healer who makes house calls. When troubles come, when sickness happens, when tempted and tested, we respond in faith to who Jesus Christ is.

The apostle Paul said whatever is not of faith is sin. That's pretty harsh isn't it? Except, when Jesus is present, faith is not difficult. The Roman soldier was in the very presence of God, so he exercised faith. It's not surprising that faith is not exercised if the presence of Jesus is not acknowledged. We respond to the presence of God by acting in faith. This will impress and please the One who makes house calls.

Adam and Eve foolishly thought they could hide the fact of sin from God but notice that God came to where they were (Genesis 3:8-19). It is true that we should "want" to draw near to God, but it is equally true that He comes to us. No one will have an excuse when they stand before the judgment seat of God because He has made a house call to everyone who has lived or will ever live.

One of the worst pains that we may experience is loneliness. It is the cause of great emotional and mental trouble. It also contributes to obesity and other physiological problems. In addition, those who do commit horrible atrocities are often found to be very lonely people. In his novel, *The Great Gatsby*, F. Scott Fitzgerald wrote:

> "The loneliest moment in someone's life is when they are watching their whole world fall apart, and all they can do is stare blankly."[105]

We are designed as social creatures and we crave connection even though it is sometimes destructive. Nothing hurts the inner man more than to be

---

[105] "The Great Gatsby," F. Scott Fitzgerald, Scribner's, 1925.

ignored. Social networks such as Twitter and Facebook have highlighted our deep ache to be known and to know others in return. Sadly, a great majority of people do not experience meaningful relationships with their families and have few, if any friends whom they take into their lives. We all deeply need the presence of God in our lives, but the better news is that Jesus Christ desires to come into our homes, and I mean more than the place where you lay your head at night. What I mean is the home of your *very life*. He wants to dwell with you in the most intimate places where no one else can. Your thoughts, the deep places of your life, are where He wants to dwell. You may say, "But I am not worthy." You would be correct! We are not worthy, but He is willing to come and heal because He is the Holy One of God.

One hundred and four times the promise of God's presence is found in scripture. The Psalmist said, "God is our refuge and strength, a very present help in trouble" (Psalm 46:1). Sometimes we may say, "I'm with you," or, "I'm behind you," although we don't say how far behind, but God is right there. He's right with you.

We can easily believe that God is transcendent, meaning that He is so great and big that He is the incomprehensible Creator existing outside of space and time, but He is also imminent. He's near.

Though Jesus physically ascended into heaven and is at the right hand of the Father right now, He is here with us by the Spirit of God. Can you get a picture of how big God is?

The apostle Paul wrote, "Rejoice in the Lord always; again, I will say, rejoice! Let your gentle spirit be known to all men. The Lord is near" (Philippians 4:4, 5). The context of this is not the second coming of Christ. Because Jesus is near, we don't have to worry. We can rejoice! To the disciples the thought of Jesus going somewhere where they could not go was very disturbing.

Wise people will join with the Psalmist when he said, "Do not banish me from your presence, and don't take your Holy Spirit from me" (Psalm 51:11). Even though mankind largely is trying to live far away from the presence of God, we desperately desire the presence of God in our lives, especially when facing trouble.

Later we will see that a result of God's presence is not only peace but is also joy. God's presence is amazing in that it doesn't always dismiss the trouble. "When David Livingstone returned to his native Scotland after sixteen difficult years as a missionary and explorer in Africa, his body was emaciated by the ravages of some twenty-seven fevers that had coursed through his veins during the years of his service. His left arm hung useless at his side, the result of his being mangled by a lion. Speaking to the students at Glasgow University, he said, 'Shall I tell you what sustained me during the hardship and loneliness of my exile? It was Christ's promise, "Lo, I am with you always, even to the end of the age."'[106]

An amazing interaction took place between the Creator and Moses. It teaches us about the nearness of God:

> "One-day Moses said to the LORD, 'You have been telling me, "Take these people up to the Promised Land." But you haven't told me whom you will send with me. You have told me, 'I know you by name, and I look favorably on you.' If it is true that you look favorably on me, let me know your ways so I may understand you more fully and continue to enjoy your favor. And remember that this nation is your very own people.' The LORD replied, 'I will personally go with you, Moses, and I will give you rest—everything will be fine for you.' Then Moses said, 'If you don't personally go with us, don't make us leave this place. How will anyone know that you look favorably on me—on me and on your people—if you don't go with us? For your presence among us sets your people and me apart from all other people on the earth.' The LORD replied to Moses, 'I will indeed do what you have asked, for I look favorably on you, and I know you by name.' Moses responded, 'Then show me your glorious presence'" (Exodus 33:12-18 NLT).

David Guzik writes, "My Presence will go with you" is literally "My Face will go with you." This helps us to understand what it means when it says Moses met with God face to face (Exodus 32:11). It has the sense of "in the immediate presence of God."[107] Contextually, Moses may not have been struggling with the kinds of problems we may face, but Moses knew that God's presence is essential when facing potential threats to the lives of His people Israel. Often, we may be tempted to believe that God has left us when we face problems and pain. After all, when Jesus was on the cross, did

---

[106] Billy Graham, op cit., Thomas Nelson Inc., Nashville TN, 2002, p.17

[107] www.blueletterbible.org/Comm/guzik_david/StudyGuide_Exd/Exd_33.cfm?a=83013

He not say, "My God, My God, why have you forsaken me?" (Matthew 27:46) Jesus had experienced incredible physical and emotional pain, but He had never known separation from His Father. Can you sense the tension? Jesus Christ, the Son of God, the second person of the Godhead, was at a horrible moment. He was separated from God the Father. Imagine for a moment just how terrible that was. Bearing your sin and mine, as well as the sins of all humanity, came between Jesus and the Father. Now imagine what that would be for eternity. Nothing, absolutely nothing, is worse than being separated from the presence of God for forever. This is called death, but we can know the presence of God even in the temporary problems that we face on this earth.

Scott Wesley Brown wrote *When Answers Aren't Enough*, a song that so beautifully describes what we are attempting to say here.

> You have faced the mountains of desperation
> You have climbed, you have fought, you have won
> But this valley that lies coldly before you
> Casts a shadow you cannot overcome
>
> And just when you thought you had it all together
> You knew every verse to get you through
> But this time the sorrow broke more than just your heart
> And reciting all those verses just won't do
>
> When answers aren't enough, there is Jesus
> He is more than just an answer to your prayer
> And your heart will find a safe and peaceful refuge
> When answers aren't enough, He is there
>
> Instead of asking why did it happen
> Think of where it can lead you from here
> And as your pain is slowly easing, you can find a greater reason
> To live your life triumphant through the tears"[108]

The presence of God is only a threat to those who despise who He is but to be forever separated from the love of God would result in the worst loneliness anyone could ever imagine and experience. Death is not a great party as some imagine.

---

[108] Scott Wesley Brown and Greg Nelson, "When Answers Aren't Enough,"1987, Greg Nelson Music and Pamela Kay Music

God's presence is an easy answer to whatever dilemma you face. We invite you to ask the Creator to come and presence Himself, not just where you are physically, but also to invite Him into your trouble. He is infinitely able to handle each problem that threatens your life. He also loves you and wants to comfort you amid the problem. Remember the Psalmist David's words, "Even though I walk through the valley of the shadow of death I fear no evil, for You are with me" (Psalm 23:4). The presence of God is your easy answer right now.

Chapter Eleven

The Glory of God or "Is God Greater Than My Problem?"

John W. Telman

An amazing story of life, suffering, death, and disappointment took place that the apostle John records. He tells us that a man named Lazarus, who was a friend of Jesus, was sick. He was so sick that he died. His sisters got word to Jesus that Lazarus was sick, but Jesus didn't come right away. In fact, scripture tells us that he *purposely* delayed going to his friends for two days (John 11:6).

Have you ever felt that God has delayed an answer to your problem? That's fair, but there may be a reason that you are not aware of. In the case of Lazarus, there were easy answers for his sisters not only about his sickness and death, but also about why Jesus didn't run to help immediately.

Some have had long-standing troubles that seem to have no end. Like children who say, "Are we there yet?" some of us struggle with delays and often ask the "why" question because we haven't experienced God's help yet.

At the tomb of Lazarus, Jesus, repeated himself and said, "If you believe, you will see the glory of God." This word that we translate as "glory" is the Greek word *doxa*, which means "brightness and magnificence." In other words, the glory of God is so powerful that it makes our troubles pale. Jesus wanted Mary, Martha (the sisters of Lazarus), the mourners, and us to know that God is greater than death and even decomposition!

The best way to illustrate the glory of God is to go outside on a sunny day and try to look at the sun in all its brilliance. We can't. If you hold any light up in comparison to the sun, it pales to the *doxa* of the sun. Picture a candle as your trouble and see the sun as God's glory, His *doxa*.

When we come to realize that the glory of God is far greater than the glory of problems, we can join with the Psalmist when he wrote, "I wait quietly before God, for my victory comes from him. He alone is my rock and my salvation, my fortress where I will never be shaken. So many enemies against one man— all of them trying to kill me. To them I'm just a broken-down wall or a tottering fence. They plan to topple me from my high position. They delight in telling lies about me. They praise me to my face but curse me in their hearts. Let all that I am wait quietly before God, for my hope is in him. He alone is my rock and my salvation, my fortress where I will not be shaken" (Psalm 62:1-6).

God is greater than cancer. He's greater than poverty. He's greater than abandonment, but we must also believe that His timing is wisest. He wants us to know that no matter how long or how difficult the problem has been, His *doxa* outshines all that we may face. His glory is our easy answer.

We all pray for the end of pain, but few allow it to leave through the power of God. Some surprisingly hang on to pain caused by unforgiveness or by doubting the love of God. Others don't want to feel the pain, so they've created so many layers in their lives to protect them from the pain. They have become hard, crusty, unfeeling, and not open to God. His way is for us to let it go by forgiving others and by totally trusting that He will show His glory even in our pain.

Corrie Ten Boom wrote, "The suffering of today cannot be compared with the glory of what is to come. It is a comfort, but meanwhile there is that certainty today, given to us by the Lord, not a spirit of fear but a spirit of love, strength, and sensibility. Because of the Holy Spirit you need not fear, even though mountains fall into the sea. Be filled with God's Spirit, who shows you that God doesn't have problems, only plans. There never is any panic in heaven. God is faithful; His plans do not fail."[109]

Have you ever asked questions like, "What are you doing God? Are you busy helping others? What are you trying to show me?" Jesus was not fearful in delaying His coming to Lazarus and He is not intimidated by our frustrations. There is no one to whom He would not come and show His glory. It's terribly sad for people to choose to stay sick or live in unforgiveness. He is willing to let trouble, trouble us until we cry out to Him in belief and trust.

---

[109] "I Stand at The Door and Knock," Corrie Ten Boom, Zondervan, 2008, p.155

Joseph was rejected by his very own family. Maybe you, too, understand that kind of pain, but the amazing reality is that Joseph forgave his brothers and did not hold a grudge. After many years Joseph became an authority over his brothers. He could have crushed them with anger and a self-righteous attitude: "They have it coming." Surprisingly, Joseph said, "Don't be afraid of me. Am I God, that I can punish you? You intended to harm me, but God intended it all for good. He brought me to this position, so I could save the lives of many people. No, don't be afraid. I will continue to take care of you and your children." So, he reassured them by speaking kindly to them" (Genesis 50:19-21).

We want you to know that no matter how bad your pain has been or currently is, God has a plan for your life and He really does care for you.

The sisters of Lazarus sent word to Jesus that the one "whom You love is sick" (John 11:3). The word they used for love was *phileo*, which is a friendship kind of love. Jesus was a friend of Lazarus, Mary and Martha but He wanted Martha to know He was more than a buddy. He was asking Martha, "Do you believe I am more than a friend? Do you believe who I am? Do you believe I *agape* you?" That means, his love is 100% giving of himself. That's the kind of love that does not change no matter what. It's the kind of love that sees you through all the brokenness of this world and it is a kind of love that gives the believer hope that others just don't have.

Jesus not only weeps when we experience pain; He absolutely loves us. So, when we ask, "Who is Jesus?" we have the answer that takes us past the temporary troubles. Remember, Jesus was not just a friend to Lazarus, Mary, and Martha. He *agaped* them! And the good news is that Jesus also has *agape* for you, too! When we were yet sinners, Christ died for us! God *agaped* the world! (John 3:16)

God is infinitely greater than our problems. You may argue that pain is greater, but the fact is that the Creator has no limit. He freely offers life and health to all who put their trust in Him. Like Mary and Martha, we need to see that God loves us even though we experience trouble.

The friends and family of Bruce Merz, about whom we spoke earlier, can tell you about the glory of God in the face of a horrible illness. You see, Bruce lay dying. His wife, Lara, wrote, "The doctor told me they found necrotizing fasciitis (flesh-eating disease) in his leg and that the surgeon had cut his leg open from behind his knee on the back of his left leg up to his bottom."[110] A perfectly healthy young man with a wife and children had become extremely ill.

Lara wrote further, "The nurse told me that they had struggled to keep Bruce alive all night. Apparently, his blood pressure plummeted rapidly even on the meds. They had added another medication and upped them both to nearly the highest doses they can give, and he just hung on with a minimal blood pressure. I was told that he nearly flatlined twice that night because he had no blood pressure on his own. His body was going into full septic shock. His kidneys were getting worse. His blood was poisoned, and because the blood flows everywhere through the body his whole system had begun to shut down."[111]

Bruce was quickly dying.

Their story deserves to be mentioned in length since it is a story showing the glory of God. Since Bruce was not aware of what was happening, Lara wrote, "There were at least two separate prayer meetings for Bruce happening at people's homes. I later found out that many other people in groups and churches around the world were also meeting to pray for Bruce. Word of his condition was spreading rapidly via social media. I had no idea how rapidly."[112] Incidentally, the church that I pastor also joined in prayer directed for Bruce's healing and we did not know him at the time, but we knew the God who is greater than flesh-eating disease.

Lara spent many hours in the ICU waiting room with many of Bruce's friends. His conditioned worsened as his kidneys failed which led to him gaining 78 pounds in three days. The situation was bleak but Lara shares what amazingly happened.

> "Though the room had chipped salmon-coloured walls and worn mismatched chairs from the nineties, it had been transformed from a cold, lonely, isolated area to a place filled 24 hours a day with people praying, singing softly, or sipping coffee-and most importantly, laughing. I cannot even express how amazing laughter is in a time like this. It

---

[110] "While He Lay Dying," Bruce Merz and Lara Merz, Essence Publishing: Belleville, ON, 2014 p.36

[111] Ibid. p.39

[112] Ibid. p.42.

might seem foreign or unloving to people reading this, but you must remember that the Lord was carrying me and our family through this time. The atmosphere in that place held such peace and joy that a nurse asked one of my friends, "Do you think Lara realizes how serious this situation is?" Yes, I realized, and at times I almost despaired, especially alone at night, but I also had a sense of love, joy, and peace that could only come from a supernatural download from God. To observers, the circumstances certainly didn't warrant it."[113]

Even though Bruce was so sick with six potentially fatal conditions all occurring at the same time, the truth that God is greater than his sickness was equally a reality. God did not change because of the situation and God has not change just because you have experienced pain. His glory outshines your problem no matter what it is.

In the middle of her ordeal Lara's young son said, "We don't hass to be afraid, Mommy. We don't hass to be afraid because Jesus is wis us! Jesus is wis us, Mommy, Jesus is wis us!!"[114] Friend, know that God is greater than your problem and that is glory is your easy answer right now.

In the middle of their grief, Mary and Martha didn't need to be afraid; instead, they needed to know the glory of God because Jesus was with them. Oh, He may have delayed so they would know, in a greater way, just who He was, but the Creator and Sustainer of life itself is not limited by His physical presence at a certain time. Death, the final enemy of life, is not as powerful as God is.

The key is to invite Jesus into your trouble and trust that He is greater. His glory outshines the darkness of your problem, no matter how dire things look, because He truly *agapes* you. No matter what is happening in your life, the glory of God is infinitely greater than the trouble and pain you are experiencing. Should He delay coming to your rescue, let faith in Him increase and fear decrease. In those waiting periods of time, know that pain is not your enemy. It certainly indicates that something is wrong, but you can find comfort in the middle of your pain as you trust the glory of God will obliterate the problem. The Psalmist wrote, "All you who fear (respect him more than anything including troubles) the LORD, trust the LORD!

---

[113] Ibid. p.46
[114] Ibid. p.51

He is your helper and your shield" (Psalm 115:11 NLT).

There is nothing so difficult, so painful, so foreboding, that can overcome the loving power of God to help anyone who simply puts their trust in Him.

Our prayer is that even as you read these words, you will be impacted by the glory of God. He is your help, and you can depend on Him. His glory is your easy answer.

Chapter Twelve

The Peace of God or "How Can I Experience Peace Right Now?"

John W. Telman

An answer to the varied issues of life is peace. We desperately want to be at peace in any situation, whether it is the health of our bodies or peace when we walk down the street. Isaiah wrote that God would keep the person whose mind is focused on God in complete peace. What an amazing and easy answer. Perfect, complete, 100% peace is available for anyone who will focus their attention on God. Isaiah wrote, "You will keep in perfect peace all who trust in you, all whose thoughts are fixed on you!" (Isaiah 26:3 NLT)

Earlier, we spoke of the fruit that God brings in our lives, even when we are facing horrible problems. Peace is one of those fruits; in some ways, it does not answer a problem, and in another way, it does.

Peace in the "midst of a storm" does not necessarily remove a problem. In fact, in many ways, troubles may remain, even when we live in peace. The peace that God grows in us get's looks. People notice how you are not shaken. It's as if the problem doesn't exist. We don't deny trouble but neither do we give in to it. People wonder why you don't turn to alcohol or put your hand through a wall when they see you facing trouble. Scott Krippayne recorded a beautiful song, *Sometimes He Calms the Storm,* that has often brought tears to my eyes.

> All who sail the sea of faith find out before too long
> How quickly blue skies can grow dark and gentle winds grow strong
> Suddenly fear is like white water pounding on the soul
> Still we sail on knowing that our Lord is in control
>
> Sometimes He calms the storm with a whispered peace be still
> He can settle any sea but it doesn't mean He will
> Sometimes He holds us close and lets the wind and waves go wild

Sometimes He calms the storm and other times He calms His child

He has a reason for each trial that we pass through in life
And though we're shaken we cannot be pulled apart from Christ
No matter how the driving rain beats down on those who hold to faith
A heart of trust will always be a quiet peaceful place[115]

Peace does not always remove the problem so how is the peace of God an easy answer? The fact is that answers are not always the absence of problems. This song reminds us of that fact, but we need to consider just what peace is.

The great English preacher Charles Spurgeon once wrote:

> "We need winds and tempests to exercise our faith, to tear off the rotten bough of self-dependence, and to root us more firmly in Christ. The day of evil reveals to us the value of our glorious hope."[116]

Even though we may drive defensively, we are not in control of the actions of others. Numerous times, my car has been hit by someone with less than good decision-making skills. The peace that God gives is one that helps us deal with what others do. Instead of anger and rage, with peace we can face problems that others cause.

Dr. James Dobson wrote:

> "What does a person do when God makes no sense? To who does he confess his troubling-even heretical-thoughts? From whom does he seek counsel? What does he tell his family when his faith is severely shaken? Where does he go to find a new set of values and beliefs? While searching for something more reliable in which to believe, he discovers that there is no other name—no other god—to whom he can turn."[117]

You may have cried out to God, "Why did you let this happen?" It's as if what He permits doesn't make sense. No other answer but God's peace will

---

[115] "Sometimes He Calms the Storm," Benton Kevin Stokes, Tony W. Wood, © Universal Music Publishing Group 1995.

[116] "Morning and Evening," Charles Spurgeon, Hendrickson Publishers, Peabody, Mass., 1995, p.240

[117] "When God Doesn't Make Sense," James Dobson, Tyndale House Publishers, Wheaton, Illinois, p.18

get anyone through tragedy. Remember Alberta Wood from the introduction to this book? She experiences the peace of God even today. It didn't bring back her son Dale, but it comforts her so that she can live the joyful life that God gave her, and, boy, does she! Few people live with such peace and joy than Alberta Wood. If you have the privilege to meet her, you will never suspect the trouble she has faced. Peace lives on her face and in her heart.

As a part of a song, the prophet Isaiah wrote, "The steadfast of mind You will keep in perfect peace, because he trusts in You" (Isaiah 26:3). It's unfortunate that many of the translators render this verse, "perfect peace," when it is better translated as, "peace." *Shalom shalom* are the original Hebrew words used. Anytime we read a word repeated in scripture, it's important to note that the writer is emphasizing what is being said. In this case, Isaiah is telling us that the mind that is constantly thinking about who God is, finds "real" peace. Complete peace. Perfect peace. Peace peace! Shalom shalom!

In a wonderful devotional book, Billy Graham wrote, "When our minds are stayed on God, we won't be worried about the future, because we know it is in His hands. We won't tremble over what might happen because our lives are built upon the solid rock of Christ.[118]Of course, that's looking forward, but when we have the past that may have been difficult, it's a challenge to look optimistically to the future. As was stated earlier, we need to focus our attention on who God is and avoid fixating on the past problems.

The apostle Paul reminded the Philippian Christians to "Rejoice in the LORD always" (Philippians 4:4), because of the nearness of God. In a previous chapter we discussed the blessing of God's presence when in trouble. Paul also encouraged his readers to, "Be anxious for nothing, but in everything by prayer and supplication with thanksgiving let your requests be made known to God. And the peace of God, which surpasses all comprehension, will guard your hearts and your minds in Christ Jesus" (Philippians 4:6-7). We learn through these verses that peace is a result of rejoicing, thanking God, and praying for help.

Peace is realized in troubled times. No one understands this better than Brian Bigam, my brother-in-law. Brian recalls a horrible period.

---

[118] op cit., Billy Graham, Thomas Nelson, Nashville TN, 2002, p. 136

"You're under arrest. You have the right to remain silent. As the police officer spoke those words, my life was about to change. I was going to start a journey I would never have dreamed about."[119]

Brian was charged with fraud. His identity was stolen and now he was told that there would be a good chance that would be found guilty. Anyone who knows Brian Bigam knows that he was innocent. Brian took the advice of the lawyers and pled to the charges. He was sentenced to 120 hours of community service, house arrest for three months, a curfew for one year and a two-year ban from the place where he worked. In addition, he had to fully pay all that was stolen from his company.

Brian stated, "Some people did not understand why I took the deal and admitted to doing something I did not do but there are times you just have to endure pain and suffering. There are different people in the Bible that were falsely accused of things but endured the suffering and they came through."

As bad as this was, there was more trouble to come. Brian was penniless, and the stress took its toll on both his and my sister's physical health and emotions. He worked two jobs but lost most income to paying off the debt. They went bankrupt three times and had to move four times because they could not pay their rent. I know how bad it was. It hurt friends and family to see them in so much pain, especially when Brian was innocent. The dark tunnel seemed unending. In fact, it lasted over ten years. "This experience taught me the importance of listening to God's voice and following his plans and purposes He has for us. From the beginning of this journey, Melody and I did not like going through it, but we did it with peace and assurance. We knew that everything would be fine, and that God had the whole thing under control. We have had many people say that they could not believe the attitude we were showing because we were so calm about everything. We made a choice to let God take care of the situation and give us peace about how to deal with it. It was not fun and yes it was challenging and yes we had moments of feeling alone but we reminded ourselves this season in our lives will pass."

The easy answer in a difficult situation was for Brian and Melody to trust God. One of their favorite verses is, "Blessed is the man who perseveres

---

[119] Brian has openly and publicly shared his story with many people.

under trial; for once he has been approved, he will receive a crown of life which the LORD has promised to those who love Him" (James 1:12). The road was not easy, but the answer was.

Brian learned a different perspective that helped him understand about the dark tunnel he had gone through: "I was walking through Churchill Square in downtown Edmonton. It was a route I had taken hundreds of times (no exaggeration). I saw some buildings and stopped to take a picture. Later that day I downloaded the pictures. There was something about one picture that for the next several days I just could not get out of my mind. Finally, I asked the LORD if there was something, He was trying to teach me. Why had I never taken this picture before if I walked this route before? Then it came to me. Usually, I would be looking straight ahead so as not to walk into someone or something but on this morning, I was looking up. I was seeing things from a different perspective. The LORD told me, in the same way I needed to view His word from a different perspective. I needed to look at it from God's perspective."

Brian could have read the words of scripture that would tell him about the peace that God has for him, but he needed to see things from a higher place. Peace was a reality through the pain and even after the pain eased.

In the 1960's, many would raise two fingers in a sign and say, "Peace, man," as if doing so would bring a healing balm. The sad fact is that to many believe peace comes from symbolic gestures. Reality hits us hard and peace seems to be something that we only read about in books, but God has an answer for you. In fact, Jesus Christ has a nickname that draws us to Him: "The Prince of Peace" (Isaiah 9:6).

The peace that all of us lack is the peace between us and God the Creator. Jesus Christ came to bridge the gap and to heal the broken relationship between mankind and God. It was humanity, and it continues to be humanity, that has made war against God. We've sinned and dismissed peace, but God in His infinite mercy sent the Son, not to condemn but to bring everlasting peace (John 3:17). This is a peace that far outweighs the squabbles that we have with family or friends. God is the initiator of peace on a global scale, and He is the one who seeks to bring peace to your troubled situation. He will bring "life" to your life as you cry out to Him in confession and repentance. Watch how He will not only bring immediate peace (even in the middle of trouble), but also notice that He will give you the kind of peace that the absence of trouble could not do.

Chapter Thirteen

The Hope of God or "Why Should I Not Give Up?"

John W. Telman

Earlier, we mentioned the 25th book of the Bible named Lamentations. In it we read that the sin of Jeremiah's people (Israel) resulted in a destroyed society. When we make a mess of our lives by turning away from God, He doesn't say, "I told you so," but continues to be the God of Hope.

Jeremiah was flooded with unbearable sorrow after the Babylonians finished destroying Jerusalem and Judah. Nothing provokes prayer like a devastating calamity, but let's not wait until tragedy strikes to pray, because God is a God of Hope. For twenty-five years, Jeremiah stood in the gap for Judah and Jerusalem, preaching, praying, and prophesying. The people resisted every effort to be saved from destruction. But even in defeat, after desolation came, and their souls were oppressed by their captors, Jeremiah never stopped pleading with God. As an aside, prayer warriors never stop praying, because He is a God of Hope. Give it twenty-five years like Jeremiah did.

There is no point to praying to a god who does not care, but we know that the Creator is the God of Hope. Jeremiah also knew this and even though things had literally crumbled around him, he still had a hope in the Creator of all things.

Things can get bad. We can mess up terribly, and life can hit us between the eyes. In those times, we are wise to focus our attention on God and then place our faith in the One who can see us through it or miraculously change things.

Grammy Award-winning singer/songwriter, Steven Curtis Chapman and his wife Mary Beth, didn't see trouble coming, but one day it came with a fury. It was a day when they should have been celebrating many things, including planning for their daughter's wedding. Sadly, an accident took the life of their young, adopted daughter Maria.

> "Maria wanted to hang from the monkey bars on their playground but wasn't tall enough to reach them on her own. When she saw her big brother Will, then 17, steering down the driveway, she darted off to meet him and ask for his help. Will never saw her coming, and fatally struck his sister with the car. The Chapman family's personal struggle in the wake of the tragedy was deep, and complex: the loss of a child, the feelings of devastated guilt gripping another."[120]

Remarkably the family, including Will, appeared on national news programs to not only share the pain but also the hope that is found in Jesus Christ. Instead of being destroyed by the events of that fateful day, they found hope. In fact, Steven and Mary Beth believe so much in adoption they founded Show Hope in 2000. It's aimed at helping families facing the financial burden of adopting a child. Thousands of families have received grants to adopt an orphan. In addition, Mary Beth wrote a beautiful book titled, *Choosing To SEE: A Journey of Struggle and Hope.*" We will quote from this touching and most powerful book a little later in this chapter.

Hope in the Bible is not the same as hoping it won't rain tomorrow. Hoping in the Bible is based on certainty. It will happen, we just haven't seen it yet. The reason we can hope in the middle of trouble is because of who the Creator is. He brings life and health, so even in the face of death and pain, we look to see who He is and are both strengthened and comforted by the hope He brings.

By now you have noticed that we often quote songs. They speak well to the topics. Those who write the songs and perform them know from experience just how deep trouble can get, and that God is our help. Philips, Craig, and Dean recorded a beautiful song, *Hope Has a Name,* that focuses on the One who gives hope while we go through the deep, dark valley of problems.

> There is a peace in the chaos there is a grace for the flame
> A strength for the battle a shield for the arrow
> A faith that endures every pain

---

[120] http://blogs.tennessean.com/tunein/2010/08/29/mary-beth-chapman-shares-%E2%80%98journey-of-struggle-and-hope%E2%80%99-in-new-book/

Our hope, our hope has a name
Jesus, Jesus is with us

He is the Hope for the patient who waits
He is the Hope for the sinner and saint
He is the Hope at the end of the day
He is the Hope who's never late[121]

Hope is based on a trusted person. It's comforting when things are difficult. Hope for the Christian is based on the truth found in this song. Hope is personified in the Lord Jesus Christ. Without Him, hope is reduced to wishful thinking. Relief may happen. You might win the lottery. A miracle might happen. These and other thoughts will go through the mind of someone who does not know that hope has a name.

No matter what problems you face, one of the three most important possessions is hope. The other two are love and faith. "Now we see in a mirror dimly, but then face to face; now I know in part, but then I will know fully just as I also have been fully known. But now faith, hope, love, abide these three; but the greatest of these is love" (1 Corinthians 13:12, 13). Remember that we often only have partial information, "We see dimly." If you lose hope, desperation sets in and can produce even more troubles. We want you to know that hope is an easy answer. It's not to be despised, but it is to be aggressively fought for.

Scripture treats hope as a sign of Christian character. When we see that God truly does love and is our help in all situations, we have hope, but it does require us to make that volitional movement towards God and to resist giving up. In a later chapter we will consider the faithfulness of God but please know that hope is a result of who God is. It is our desire to stir up your hope in who God is no matter how difficult the problem you face.

Mary Beth writes the following in, *Choosing To SEE: A Journey of Struggle and Hope*. Let these words inspire you to hope from a woman who knows about pain and suffering but also knows about hope:

"I so desperately long to heal from so much pain . . . missing my sweet Maria. Trying to find the meaning and purpose for how I will live from here on out. If we keep our heads down, either out of defeat or loss or shame or tiredness . . . whatever the reason, we are going to miss the

---

[121] Hope Has A Name," Philips Craig and Dean from the Album, *Above It All*, 2014.

beautiful sun (and Son) that is right there in from of us, shining its warmth on our faces and our souls! He is going to tell us where to step and when to look down if our faces are on Him. God allows the hard places of suffering and difficulties. We all have them! But if our faces are turned toward Him, He will tell us when to look and how to survive those times by completely trusting Him. He navigates the steps and takes us where He wants us to go because He loves us and wants us to become more like Him. I hope that in some this has touched or helped you. I hope that my journey will be one that will encourage you to walk . . . chin up!"[122]

Hope comes out of the experiences of pain and trouble if we will remember to reach out to the One who loves us and understands. A man who had his fair share of trouble, the apostle Paul, wrote, "Having been justified by faith, we have peace with God through our Lord Jesus Christ, through whom also we have obtained our introduction by faith into this grace in which we stand; and we rejoice in hope of the glory of God. And not only this, but we also rejoice in our tribulations, knowing that tribulation brings about perseverance; and perseverance, proven character; and proven character, hope; and hope does not disappoint, because the love of God" (Romans 5:1-5).

Maybe you're saying something like, "I followed you until the rejoicing in the middle of trouble" thing. You may have expected that it's possible to rejoice in hope, but to rejoice in tribulations? Again, we don't deny the pain and sorrow when experiencing problems, but we can hope in the One who is able to do more than we can ask or think (Ephesians 3:20), which is a joyful result. Being joyful in trouble? Yes! Hope in God will do something supernatural. Crankiness or having a pity-party will not happen when you take the step to place your hope in the One who loves you.

Mary Beth, speaking of her husband wrote, "Sometimes Steven would go up to his home studio, which is soundproof and scream as loud as he could, "Blessed be the name of the LORD! He gives and takes away! Blessed be the name of the LORD."[123] This is what Job cried out in his pain (Job 1:21). These men knew that even while suffering, God is worthy

---

[122] "Choosing to See: A Journey of Struggle and Hope," Mary Beth Chapman, Ellen Santilli Vaughn, Revell Publishing, Oregon City: OR, 2011, p. 224, 225.

[123] Ibid. p. 190.

of praise! He is the God of Hope!

Let's now speak specifically about this God of Hope.

The apostle Paul wrote much about the Creator, including that God is the God of Hope. "I pray that God, the source of hope, will fill you completely with joy and peace because you trust in him. Then you will overflow with confident hope through the power of the Holy Spirit" (Romans 15:13 NIV).

Can you see just how important hope is? A lack of hope will make the heart (not the physical organ) sick (Proverbs 13:12). It's not optional if you desire an easy answer. Incidentally, hope is *not* equal to desire. Hope is intimately wrapped in the inescapable fact that God is the One who is your answer. He's greater than all pain, all sources of pain, and He's greater than the time it takes to be healed of the suffering.

> "There are two ways God can enable us to cope with suffering: He can completely remove the pain by answering our prayers every time we ask him to remove an obstacle. But think about that. Today perhaps it is a broken arm. Tomorrow it may be a bankrupt relative. The next day it could be a dying loved one. Problems will forever remain intrinsic to the human scene. Do we play God and demand that the evil be removed at every occurrence? That is asking for the logically impossible if love is to be supreme; God doesn't want us to love Him for what we can get from Him. The other way God enables us to cope with suffering is to change us from within. He changes our hearts and walks with us through the deep waters. This is the greater miracle when compared to the mere changing of circumstances. Only a change within us can keep intact Paul's three excellencies of faith, hope and love."[124]

The God of Hope is your easy answer, no matter what situation you're facing. Mary Beth and Steven Curtis Chapman can tell you hope comes when you trust in the One who will not disappoint.

---

[124] "Why Suffering," Ravi Zacharias and Vince Vitale, Faith Words, Brentwood: TN, p.53, 2014.

Chapter Fourteen

The Wisdom of God or "Does God Know What He's Doing?"

John W. Telman

arlier we quoted Dr. James Dobson from his wonderful book, *When God Doesn't make Sense*. In it, he succeeds in helping the reader to see that God is our help in trouble. Instead of blaming God, which is a tendency for many of us, we should heed the words of Dr. Dobson when he says, "For the heartsick, bleeding soul out there today who is desperate for a word of encouragement, let me assure you that you can trust this Lord of heaven and earth."[125] God is wise in every sense of the word. Instead of blaming Him for what has happened, we should seek the easy answer found in his wisdom.

Are you there right now? Do you wonder if God knows what He's doing? Dr. Dobson continues, "After years of consistent answers to prayers, the Lord may choose not to grant a request we think is vitally important. In a matter of moments, the world can fall off its axis. Panic stalks the soul as life and death hang in the balance. A pounding heart betrays the anxiety within."[126]

The frustration can be so overwhelming that even a Christian can despair. In case you are currently feeling that God's, wisdom escapes you, we want you to know that you're in good company. Many people through human history have questioned what is happening.

John the Baptist was in prison after being obedient to God and even though he stated that Jesus was "the Lamb of God who takes away the sin of the world" (John 1:29), he sat in a horrible Roman prison asking if Jesus really was the "Expected One" (Luke 7:19). Dr. Dobson writes, "My concern is

---

[125] op cit., James Dobson, Tyndale House Publishers, Wheaton, Illinois, p.21, 2012.
[126] Ibid p. 26.

that many believers apparently feel God owes them smooth sailing or at least a full explanation (and perhaps an apology) for the hardships they encounter."[127]

Does God know what He's doing? Does He really have wisdom that can help me through this problem? These are legitimate questions that will be answered fully when we recognize just who the Creator is.

Maybe you have asked, "If God is wise, why would He allow such pain in my life?" If you have thought or asked this question, you're not alone. Job's friends could not understand that God would allow Job to experience such terrible trouble if he was not guilty of some terrible sin and experiencing God's wrathful judgment. Job answered them by saying, regarding God, "With Him are wisdom and might; To Him belong counsel and understanding" (Job 12:13).

In 1967, a young woman was paralyzed in an accident when she dove into Chesapeake Bay. Joni Eareckson writes, "My accident was not a punishment for my wrongdoing-whether or not I deserved it. Only God knows why I was paralyzed."[128] She has learned valuable truths, including the following: "I understood why (the apostle) Paul could rejoice in suffering, why James could welcome trials as friends, and why Peter did not think it strange in the testing of your faith. These pressures and difficulties had ultimate positive ends and resulted in praise, honor, and glory to Christ. Circumstances have been placed in my life for cultivating my character and conforming me to reflect Christ-like qualities. And there is another purpose. Second Corinthians 1:37 explains it in terms of our being able to comfort others facing the same kinds of trials. Wisdom is trusting God, not asking 'Why God?' Relaxed and in God's will, I know He is in control. It is not a blind, stubborn, stoic acceptance, but getting to know God and realizing He is worthy of my trust. Although I am fickle and play games, God does not; although I have been up and down, bitter and doubting, He is constant, ever-loving."[129]

---

[127] Ibid p. 40, 41.
[128] "Joni," Joni Eareckson, Zondervan Corp., Grand Rapids, Mich., p.176.
[129] Ibid p. 176, 177.

God is wise! Even when we don't understand. The easy answer to paralysis and trouble of any kind is to decide that we don't have all the information, but God does. Our part is to trust Him.

God, through the prophet, said, "My thoughts are not your thoughts, neither are your ways My ways," declares the LORD. For [as] the heavens are higher than the earth, so are My ways higher than your ways, and My thoughts than your thoughts" (Isaiah 55:8-9). The good news is that "if any of you lacks wisdom, let him ask of God, who gives to all men generously and without reproach, and it will be given to him" (James 1:5).

God doesn't just know all things. His knowledge can be summarized by saying that He "knows how." No matter what we face and no matter how painful the trouble is, God has all the facts. We are wise to talk to Him about what's happened.

Trouble and the pain that comes with it, as we have earlier stated, is sometimes caused by our foolishness. Other times it is terribly random. You could be driving through a green light only to be hit by someone running a red light. The foolishness of the other driver impacted you, literally and figuratively. Could God in His wisdom warn you to go another route to avoid the collision? Yes! If we are quick to hear the prompting of God, we could often stave off trouble and pain. All too often we ignore God's wisdom and proudly go through our day not realizing that God truly desires to direct us in safe and peaceful ways.

In the book, *Why Suffering*, Vince Vitale reminds us that we are complicit in many of our troubles.

> "It is the most telling reality that by eating of the tree of the knowledge of good and evil, we uprooted that tree and today, in the day of environmental protection, all trees are protected except that one. We want to hold God accountable to our notion of good, but we want to do away with the notion of evil and be accountable to nobody. We use our freedom to try to free ourselves from the very One who gives us our freedom. We want the gift without the giver. The symptom of evil remains-suffering-but we expunge the cause of evil-our own responsibility."[130]

---

[130] "Why Suffering? Finding Meaning and Comfort When Life Doesn't Make Sense," Vince Vitale, Ravi Zacharias, Faith Works, 2014. p. 41

Again, we say God truly desires to direct us in safe and peaceful ways. Some may counter, "Can we say that is always the case? Does God, in His infinite wisdom, allow trouble?" Again, the easy answer is, "yes." God, in His wisdom, allows trouble. "Is eliminating pain always the loving thing to do? Is it a quid pro quo that if you love somebody you will make their life totally free from pain? Taking it a step further, does love always mean giving one the freedom to have or do whatever one wishes? Is it love to remove boundaries? Very quickly one can see that every premise as stated or implied by the critic makes assumptions that are actually irrational."[131]

Earlier, we mentioned that God allowed three men to be placed in a fiery furnace. Hananiah, Mishael and Azariah were threatened with death if they would not worship an idol. Their trust was completely in God, so that they answered the King with confidence. "Our God whom we serve is able to deliver us from the furnace of blazing fire; and He will deliver us out of your hand, O King. But even if He does not, let it be known to you, O King that we are not going to serve your gods or worship the golden image that you have set up" (Daniel 3:17, 18). Isn't it possible that these men knew that if they were not delivered, God knew better?

It is a spiritual discipline to resist making a rash judgment when we have less than all the information. The truth is that we may never fully have our questions answered but that does not eliminate the truth that God is wiser. Trusting God is intricately connected to finding the easy answer of wisdom.

One impediment to wisdom is what the Bible calls, "the flesh." Although the physical appetites are most often involved, we are not talking about your body. The flesh as is found in the Bible is the former manner of living prior to meeting and surrendering our lives to Jesus Christ. The apostle Paul wrote, "The mind set on the flesh is death, but the mind set on the Spirit is life and peace" (Romans 8:6). The Greek word that He used for "flesh" is *sarx* which is used 147 times in the New America Standard Version of the Bible. While there are times it's used to describe the physical body, here and in Romans 8:7 as well as in 9:10 it refers to the carnal state we were in prior to Jesus.

Struggling through the troubles of this life are made more difficult when

---

[131] Ibid. p. 8

the old manner of living directs a response. As an example, the old John likes to encourage me to not forgive when wronged. Succumbing to this temptation is not only sin, but also unwise. God's wisdom is not given to those who blatantly give in to selfish and self-serving reactions. As was stated earlier, we can sometimes make things worse. Giving in to the carnal old ways is equal to turning away from God, who desires to provide His wisdom. It's so insidious that the apostle Paul writes, "Those who belong to Christ Jesus have nailed the passions and desires of their sinful nature to his cross and crucified them there" (Galatians 5:24 NLT). While I do not hold to a "sinful nature" since it weakens our responsibility for sin, this translation helps us see just how horrible it would be to live apart from the wisdom of God.

God is the creator of all that is. He knows how things work. He's not into "cramping your style" or keeping you from having "fun." His wisdom guides you so that you can avoid problems, but His wisdom is also perfect. It's not just His opinion but for life it's the only way to approach every problem that shows up in your life. Who knows better? You? Me? Hosts of talk shows? Of course not. His knowledge of all is complete. "True wisdom and power are found in God; counsel and understanding are his" (Job 12:13). Wisdom is frequently missing from lives especially when hurting from injury, but wisdom is something that we can obtain as we humble ourselves.

Have you ever regretted a decision? Did you wish you had prayed and listened to wise counsel from godly people? Not only is it wisdom to be wise, it's your answer, your easy answer to the troubles of the past and also to what is yet to come upon you. God's wisdom is not just the wisdom of a sage who sits on top of a mountain, it's so much more. It's the path of guidance that God wants to give you. Even if you are not suffering right now, you need God's wisdom. In fact, you may need it more right now. God's wisdom may avert many harmful and destructive events in your life. We urge you to ask God to guide your decisions and to give you His wisdom in all facets of your life. You will be surprised how safe and secure you will be in the comfort of His wisdom, even if you experience great challenges.

Dr. Charles Swindoll writes:

"Wisdom is not simply a theoretical, sterile subject to be tossed around by philosophers and intellectuals. Neither is it merely a theological concept to be discussed along cloistered seminary hallways. It is practical. It's designed to work for us. Our definition makes that clear. Wisdom is the God-given ability to see life with rare objectivity and to handle life with rare stability. The good news is that such wisdom is ours to claim through an intimate relationship with God's Son, Jesus. He is the channel through which wisdom comes to us. In coming by faith to the Lord Jesus Christ, we are given open access to the wisdom of God. With the Son of God comes the wisdom of God. It's all part of the package."[132]

Our aim is to point you, the reader, to the God of all wisdom who knows better than anyone how to deal with your trouble. To see an end to your trouble that avoids the creation of other troubles, your easy answer is found in the wisdom of God. Seek Him through a close relationship with Jesus Christ.

---

[132] "Living on The Ragged Edge," Chuck Swindoll, Thomas Nelson, Nashville: TN, p. 230, 231, 2005.

Chapter Fifteen

The Faithfulness of God or "Can I Depend on God Right Now?"

John W. Telman

The faithfulness of God is one of the easiest answers to any problem. It causes us to have hope in the middle of a hard or painful time. Remember that dealing with an issue is most often just getting through it. It's true that sometimes God will miraculously heal or eliminate problems instantly, but often His desire is to walk with you through the problem. The Psalmist David wrote, "Even when I walk through the darkest valley, I will not be afraid, for you are close beside me" (Psalm 23:4 NLT). Like traveling through a long dark tunnel with a friend, it's comforting to know that the Creator is faithfully seeing you to an end of the trouble.

My wife and I took a graduate course on the book of Psalms and had our eyes opened to the faithfulness of God. The professor introduced us to a Hebrew word that is found 176 times in the Old Testament. Most often it's translated into the English word, "loving kindness." You will find it often used in the Psalms. While this sounds wonderful, its only part of how this word reveals the character of God. The word is *Hesed* which represents God's covenantal love.

Israel was the object of the covenant made by God to be faithful. The promises God made were not made with conditions. God chose Israel to be His representative in the world, but they miserably failed. The result was that over its history, Jerusalem, its capital, has been destroyed at least twice, besieged 23 times, attacked 52 times, and captured and recaptured 44 times.

Like Israel, all of us have told God, "I can do it better than You," and have shipwrecked our lives. God faithfully did not give up on us and continued to pursue us with love, compassion, and patience.

As we have stated frequently, not all problems are created by us, but some are. Even though it's true, if we would admit it, God has not given up on us. This chapter will speak to the problems that we create and to the truth that a faithful God is the easy answer to everything we have done in shame.

The mere existence of Israel is a testament to a faithful God. In fact, there is a book in the Old Testament that is all about the faithfulness of God.

Hosea was a godly man whom God told to do something very peculiar. He told Hosea to marry a beautiful girl. The strange part was that the girl he was going to marry was a prostitute and that she would not remain faithful to him. What's worse is that they would have children, three children, but she would still turn back to prostitution. Why would God instruct a godly man to do something so strange? We can answer that question by looking at the desperate situation Israel was in. Hosea was called by God to preach repentance, but people didn't pay much attention to Hosea. He said that God was going to raise up the Assyrian nation to punish Israel for their wickedness and unfaithfulness, but the people paid little attention to him; they said that Hosea's God must be vengeful to have His prophet say such things. Hosea tried to tell them that wasn't so. He said God was a God of love and that His doing this was the very activity of love; he said that God wanted them to see what they were doing to themselves, and that the only way He could get them to listen was to make things rough for them. This was theoretically to cause the people to seek God for help, but they didn't pay any more attention than people do today about things like that. Instead, they blamed God and said, "If God is really a God of love, then why does He let things get in such a mess? How could a God of love ever send a ruthless people like the Assyrians down upon our land?" Sound like what people think and say now?

There are some today who blame God for liver failure, after drinking for decades and destroying their bodies with alcohol or blame God for emphysema after chain smoking. God gets blamed even though mankind ignores His words of instruction, love, and life.

We've previously quoted Mark Mittelberg from his book, *The Questions Christians Hope No One Will Ask*, and once again, he gives us a perspective on how God permits pain in our lives for a greater purpose. "He (God) can use pain to lead us to himself. I heard an extreme example of this principal years ago from Ron, a friend at my church, who had visited a man in the hospital with a recently discovered brain cancer. At first bitter and angry at

God, this man gradually came to see that he would have never stopped ignoring God were it not for contracting this terrible disease. After several visits and lots of reflection, this man finally gave his life to Christ. He said to Ron, with tears in his eyes, that he could now totally accept the cancer because it was his only way to find God's love. The two men even prayed together, thanking God for the disease that led to salvation. That man is in heaven today because of the pain God allowed to enter his life."[133]

God's goal is not distance between His creation and Him. He will even allow brain cancer to happen for the pain to thrust us toward His loving and healing hands. You might counter that you have relationship with Him so, "Why can't pain and suffering be a thing of the past?" The problem of that question is two-fold: First, we are not perfected yet, except through trials. Even Jesus learned through trials (Hebrews 5:8). Second, we live in an imperfect world. You might ask, "Why doesn't God just make it perfect"? He did, but humans messed it up, plus there is a coming day of change when God, in His wisdom and timing, will once again make this world perfect. Until then, we are totally dependent on the love of God. Not a bad proposition if you really think about it.

Hosea's love for his unfaithful wife was to be a picture of God's faithful love for Israel which was unfaithful to Him. Through the prophet, God said to unfaithful Israel, "I will make you my wife forever, showing you righteousness and justice, unfailing love and compassion. I will be faithful to you and make you mine, and you will finally know me as the LORD" (Hosea 2:19, 20).

Another prophet wrote, "I shall make mention of the loving kindnesses (*heced*) of the Lord, the praises of the Lord, according to all that the Lord has granted us, And the great goodness toward the house of Israel, which He has granted them according to His compassion, And according to the multitude of His loving kindnesses ("*heced*" - Isaiah 63:7).

So, you may ask, "What does this have to do with my problems?" The covenantal love of God is important to your pursuit of an easy answer in that it reveals just who God really is. If you have messed things up in your life, and cannot seem to find an answer, God has an easy answer for you: It

---

[133] "The Questions Christians Hope No One Will Ask," Mark Mittelberg, Tyndale House Publishers, Carol Stream: IL, 2010, p. 152.

is that is that He is faithful. You may ask, "Faithful to what?"

God is faithful to Himself. By now you are getting a picture of God. He is good. He loves you and has promised to help you, if you only turn to Him in repentance, which simply means turning to Him and away from your decisions that got you into the trouble. He doesn't condemn because He is faithful. He doesn't change. His desire is to fix, to heal, to give life and to bless. Our response must be submission to Him. Then and only then will we find His loving kindness (*heced*) pouring over our lives.

You see, the faithfulness of God is an easy answer. We don't have to do anything except give up to His control over our lives. That may sound like much effort to some. Surrender can be difficult but not impossible. Soldiers surrender when they see the enemy has prevailed. See that God has prevailed. The difference is that He's prevailed with love. When you see He has, in fact, captured your heart, surrender. Give up. You will find His help when you do. He is faithful to complete what He started in you. That's speaking not only to His ability and power, but also to His heart of patience.

To the Corinthians, the apostle Paul encouraged them with these words, "No temptation has overtaken you, but such as is common to man; and God is faithful, who will not allow you to be tempted beyond what you are able, but with the temptation will provide the way of escape also, so that you will be able to endure it" (1 Corinthians 10:13).

The apostle Paul also wrote the Thessalonian Church and reminded them that God is faithful (1 Thessalonians 5:24). They were an early group of Christians who were experiencing extreme pain and persecution. It would have been a temptation to give up on God when trouble came, but Paul told them that God is faithful.

The Psalmist David wrote, "Do not let me fall into their hands. For they accuse me of things I've never done; with every breath they threaten me with violence. Yet I am confident I will see the LORD's goodness while I am here in the land of the living. Wait patiently for the LORD. Be brave and courageous. Yes, wait patiently for the LORD" (Psalm 27:12-14). David found courage in the face of great trouble as he reminded himself that God is faithful. Notice that because of the faithfulness of God, David found that he could wait.

We often look for answers immediately, but the faithfulness of God dismisses this demand. God is faithful, so it's not necessary to put Him on a timetable. In addition, we frustrate ourselves by watching the clock. I'm probably the worst offender, but maybe you anxiously wait for an answer, too. In addition, we may wait anxiously for what we think the answer should be. As we have previously stated, God has all the information, so complete trust in His timing is paramount. God is faithful. The sooner we accept this easy answer, the sooner we can exhale.

Dr. George Wood wrote,

> "Some months ago, I was awakened in the evening. About three in the morning, I'd had a very vivid dream. In this dream some acquaintances of ours saw this giant boulder descending upon their home. It was like a stone mountain and it was coming down out of the sky in the night hours to crush their home. That was the state of the dream when I awakened, and I sensed it was the Spirit telling me to spend some time interceding for this family. So out of the bed to spend some time praying for a family facing a danger of which I did not know. To this day I do not know what it may have been. But as I reflected upon that imagery of that dream further it seemed to me that there were two aspects of it. In their case the stone did not land on the house. But even if it had landed on the physical structure, I sensed in looking deeper into the vision that they were protected. Underneath all the rubble that would have been they would have emerged safe. That seems to be very descriptive of God's faithfulness to us. That he doesn't always create a plastic bubble of protection over our existence so that nothing comes crashing through. But he will guarantee us that when all debris of the trouble and the wreck we've been wrestling with has been cleared away we've emerged safe, secure, strengthened, unscathed."[134]

The challenge to receive the easy answer of God's faithfulness is trusting in His wisdom regarding what we can handle. He knows better than we do.

Thomas Chisholm wrote one of the most beautiful and loved hymns that has endured for decades. It is often sung at funerals. *Greatest is thy Faithfulness* was written by Chisholm when he was 75 years old, but he also wrote, "My income has not been large at any time due to impaired health in the earlier

---

[134] Sermons.georgeowood.com/faithfuless_of_god

years which has followed me on until now. Although I must not fail to record here the unfailing faithfulness of a covenant-keeping God and that He has given me many wonderful displays of His providing care, for which I am filled with astonishing gratefulness."[135]

> Another beautiful old hymn says it better than we can:
> Be not dismayed whate'er betide, God will take care of you.
> Beneath His wings of love abide, God will take care of you.
> God will take care of you,
> Thru ev'ry day, O'er all the way;
> He will take care of you, God will take care of you.
>
> Thru days of toil when heart doth fail, God will take care of you.
> When dangers fierce your path assail, God will take care of you.
> All you may need He will provide, God will take care of you.
> Nothing you ask will be denied, God will take care of you.
> No matter what may be the test, God will take care of you.
> Lean, weary one, upon His breast, God will take care of you.[136]

Have you heard the saying, "Promises are made to be broken?" This may be true for a politician or a used car salesman, but not for God. He makes promises to be kept, not with the hope of leveraging more power. He does so to show that He is pure and holy. He does as He says. He wants to prove to you and me that He is just who He is, and that there is no one who can bring a charge to Him. He is faithful and will prove it.

We urge you to not only believe that God is faithful, but also to trust Him during your trials. He has showed unmatched faithfulness to His creation and to all who will look to Him for easy answers. His answer of His faithfulness is waiting for you

---

[135] http://www.sermoncentral.com/sermons/the-faithfulness-of-god-robert-massey-sermon-on-god-the-father-47539.asp
[136] Civilla D. Martin, 1904, Public Domain

Chapter Sixteen

The Goodness of God or "Why do bad Things Happen to Good People?"

Kerry Pocha

When we speak of "the goodness of God" we are speaking of God's character, but God doesn't have characteristics like we do. We say He has characteristics so that we can understand Him like we would another human. God, however, is not like us. We are like Him. We are made by Him, in His image. God has attributes that do not change. We have characteristics which resemble God's attributes. God is not good because His acts line up with our definition of what is good, that is how we determine if another human is good, or rather, has a good character. No, I am not going to show how you can trust God because His actions line up with what you expect from a good being. Why? Because He needs no defence. God IS good in the same way that water IS wet.

If I were drinking a glass of water, and you were thirsty, you would not say, "I am so thirsty! How wet is that water you are drinking?" You may have a lot of drinks to choose from: coffee, tea, alcohol, etc., but we define how wet (or moist) something is by how much water it contains or absorbs. Religions can be like that. They provide people with a tasty substitute for the pure thing. Most religions act like vodka or coffee: they come across as thirst-quenching and godly, but the hidden additives end up causing dehydration. We define good and evil, then make rules to follow so we can determine if something is good or evil. Following a set of rules may be easier than having a relationship with God and His Son, but those rules may also interfere with our relationship with God. Jesus said, "Don't look for shortcuts to God. The market is flooded with sure fire, easygoing formulas for a successful life that can be practised in your spare time. Don't fall for that stuff, even though crowds of people do. The way to life—to God! —is vigorous and requires total attention" (Matthew 7:13-14 MSG).

Perhaps you are thinking, "Sports drinks can hydrate better than water alone." Some specialty sports drinks are designed to help our bodies get hydrated. They don't actually give our bodies more moisture than water, they simply help our bodies absorb the water in the drink faster. I am describing water and sports drinks, because that is what John and I are trying to do in this book: Help people absorb who God is, quicker and more efficiently. We are not trying to convert you to our denominations, give you ways to be more religious or even be godlier. We are trying to help you get to know our good God better, because you cannot get anything good without God.

If you are an atheist, you may disagree. A popular atheist slogan in Canada is, "I don't need god to be good." Whenever I hear it said or see it written, I am dumbfounded. It is like someone telling me they don't need water to be wet. Sure, you could splash some liquid that has no water in it, like an acid, on yourself and appear wet, but it is only an appearance of water. In art I will put a glossy coat of lacquer over a water scene to heighten its appearance of being wet, but the painting is not actually wet, it is dry. Jesus also got frustrated with such attitudes of being good without God. He said: "Blind guides! You strain a fly out of your drink but swallow a camel! How terrible for you… You hypocrites! You clean the outside of your cup and plate, while the inside is full of what you have gotten by violence and selfishness. Blind Pharisee! Clean what is inside the cup first, and then the outside will be clean too!" (Matthew 23:24a-26 GNT)

Some people say that God must not be good because the world does not seem good to them. For their next amazing trick, these logic magicians will probably stand in a desert and deny water as being wet because their surroundings are so dry! God doesn't ACT good, He IS good. God defines what good is just as water defines what wet is.

It has been said that everyone is either coming out of a hard time, in a hard time, or about to have a hard time. Likewise, everyone has either just quenched their thirst, is thirsty or is about to be thirsty. Are you thirsty? Drink water. Are you dry? Jump into some water. Short of good things in your life? Get to know God better. Absorb Him into your life, immerse yourself in who He is. Don't be content with just looking good or having "good things" in your life. Stop looking for the gifts God can give and begin enjoying the Giver of every good gift. Drink God in and bathe in His presence. Think about God and who He is round-the-clock. Some people carry around a water bottle to stay hydrated. Begin carrying around a Bible to stay "God-rated." Try hearing from God as often as you have something to drink. Talk to God, read what He has to say in His Word, discuss Him with others, tell everyone about the good things God has done in your life, and worship Him constantly. Try listening to only Christian radio and worship music for a month and see the difference it makes in your attitude. Bathe in His presence. When you know He is near (such as at church), soak it in. Relax and absorb the warm love of His Holy Spirit.

When it comes to having God in our lives, too many of us act like medieval farmers. Instead of drawing a bath, or showering, every day, we think bath day is an awkward obligation we only have to do once or twice a year. Do you only shower once a week, month, or year? Do you only drink liquids once you are so dehydrated you have a headache and can't even stomach water? Not likely. No one likes feeling sick or dirty, yet we try to go days without trying to hear God. We wait even longer to have Him surround us with His presence. It feels good to be clean and well-hydrated, but we have to change our attitudes toward having God's goodness in our lives.

Our attitude can be defined as the outward manifestation of an internal belief or struggle. In other words, what we truly believe is true, is what we will act on. God's Son said, ". . . Anyone who intends to come with me has to let me lead. You're not in the driver's seat; I am. Don't run from suffering; embrace it. Follow me and I'll show you how. Self-help is no help at all. Self-sacrifice is the way, my way, to saving yourself, your true self. What good would it do to get everything you want and lose you, the real you? What could you ever trade your soul for?" (Mark 8:34-37 MSG)

Two thousand years later, science has caught up with the Bible. A modern psychiatrist, Abigail Brenner, put it like this:

> "Your beliefs create and dictate what your attitudes are. Your attitudes create and dictate how you respond—in other words, they dictate your feelings. And your feelings largely determine how you behave . . .Many of you who have been in therapy would probably say that your experience helped you gain insights, acquire tools, and develop skills to help you cope better. But many would also have to say that being in therapy, as well as reading self-help/self-improvement books, and attending seminars, while often interesting and inspirational, did not provide the long-term benefits that can only come from real change.

And that means changing your core beliefs. Without that, it's simply on to the next therapy and on to the next self-help book."[137]

So, psychology agrees with Jesus that "Self-help is no help at all." We must change our core beliefs of who God is. We need to know that God is the definition of good.

It has been said that people are like tea bags – you don't really know whether they are any good until you put them in hot water. Too often, we concern ourselves with removing our symptoms rather than dealing with the cause of our pain. We are often like an alcoholic, who simply wants to keep drinking while avoiding the headaches and drunk driving charges. Rather than let go of the belief that we can control all outcomes in our lives, we spend our lives and resources on aspirin, taxis, and booze, and maintain our illusion (or delusion) of control. God wants us to give Him control over our core beliefs.

A core belief that God IS good will fundamentally change what comes out of you in every situation. How we view our suffering, for instance, is determined by our view of God. The larger we see our problems, the smaller God seems, but the larger God is to us, the smaller our problems seem. God's Son viewed His upcoming, excruciating death this way: "Listen carefully: Unless a grain of wheat is buried in the ground, dead to the world, it is never any more than a grain of wheat. But if it is buried, it sprouts and reproduces itself many times over. In the same way, anyone who holds on to life just as it is destroys that life. But if you let it go, reckless in your love, you'll have it forever, real and eternal. If any of you wants to serve me, then follow me. Then you'll be where I am, ready to serve at a moment's notice. The Father will honor and reward anyone who serves me" (John 12:24-26 MSG).

Jesus also told a parable of a field, where two types of seed were sown. The farmer planted good seed. Then an enemy came at night and planted weeds. The workers wanted to tear up the weeds, but the farmer said not to, "because while you are pulling the weeds, you may uproot the wheat with them. Let both grow together until the harvest. At that time, I will tell the harvesters: First collect the weeds and tie them in bundles to be burned;

---

[137] Posted November 12, 2012 on https://www.psychologytoday.com/blog/in-flux/201211/you-are-what-you-believe by Abigail Brenner, M.D.

then gather the wheat and bring it into my barn" (Matthew 13:29-31 NIV).

We all know that wages are not reckoned until the work is done. Once the work is finished, the owner deducts expenses, taxes, breakage, etc., then we net what is left over. When we ask, "Why do bad things happen to good people?" we are asking for a fair wage for everyone's efforts—right now! But your work isn't over; neither is theirs, so stop asking for wages. If we ask for our wages while we still have work to do, we are asking to quit and go home, and no one really wants that.

God is good—all the time. Even when we cannot see it. Let me tell you a parable: Twins were born into a good home, but it soon became obvious to both children that their father favoured one over the other. Every day, the first child opened another present while their sibling watched. Each day, they taunted their sibling with their many gifts, refusing to share, secure that they were the father's favourite and would never be disciplined.

One day, the second child got a gift, but it looked interesting, so the first child demanded it and their father instructed the second child to share. "I hate this place!" screamed the second child, who dropped the toy, and ran to their room. The father followed them shortly after and sat on the edge of the bed until the poor kid couldn't cry any more. "I have more bad news for you," he began. "You were too immature to understand, but now you need to know."

The second twin said, "What could possibly be worse than living here? Everything is so unfair!"

"More than you know, actually. You see—this is not your home. This is more of a hospital than a home. I built it when you were born. When you were babies, an enemy of mine poisoned you both with a contagious disease. I developed a cure and every day I tried to give you each the antidote with an eyedropper. You accepted each dose, but your brother has always been obstinate, and refused the medicine, spitting it back up every time. After a while, it was too late, the virus had taken him, and I had to give up. You were cured, and he was not.

"I love you both so much, but every day I see the two of you I know there will soon be only one. Every gift I give your brother is with the knowledge that he only has a few more weeks to play with it, then it will be yours forever. Every day I spend with each of you in this place is with the knowledge that when you leave here you are going to two quite different places. You will come with me to a mansion I have built specially for you, and your brother will go to a small box in a very deep hole. I know. It's not fair. You don't get many presents and your brother is selfish and seldom genuinely nice, but he doesn't understand what you do now. I leave it up to you to decide how you are going to act, now that you know, but I was wondering . . . could you help me show your brother how much I love you both, while there is still a little time left to do so?"

The easy answer to, "If God is good, then why do good things happen to 'bad' people?" or its sister question, "Why do bad things happen to 'good' people?" is that our Father in Heaven loves us all and knows where we are all going. Our time here is short, and our wages will be better than fair, but our Father is asking, "Could you help me show your brother how much I love you both, while there is still a little time left to do so?"

Now that you understand that God *is* good, will you determine to obey Him with your heart and soul, every day, forever? Go to "You are Invited," and accept Jesus, God's Son, as your Saviour, your cure, to the "sin cancer" infecting you. Commit (or re-commit) yourself to looking at this poor world as the hospital it is, and at its inmates as your brothers. Let the dying have their toys and share freely, all your gifts, with both the sick and the well.

> "So don't be misled, my dear brothers and sisters. Whatever is good and perfect is a gift coming down to us from God our Father, who created all the lights in the heavens. He never changes or casts a shifting shadow. He chose to give birth to us by giving us his true word. And we, out of all creation, became his prized possession" (James 1: 16-18 NLT).

Conclusion

John W. Telman

My wife can tell you that I have much disdain for commercials that propose easy ways to lose weight. It appears to me that somehow the word *easy* is supposed to make the product legitimate. Possibly we are lazy and don't want the daily struggle of watching calories and exercising. *Easy* may appeal to our fleshly ways that resist responsibility. There may be more reasons to avoid the word "easy," but in terms of engaging God, we must realize that God alone has the answers. There are no gray areas with God's way. In a very real sense, God offers easy answers, since there is only one way for truth, and that way is God's way.

Even though we say answers are easy through God, we are not denying the presence and impact of problems and pain. The late Rich Mullins wrote a song, *Bound to Come Some Trouble*, that so accurately describes the fact that problems exist, but that they do not have to be fatal because of who God is.

> There's bound to come some trouble to your life
> But that ain't nothing to be afraid of
> There's bound to come some trouble to your life
> But that ain't no reason to fear
>
> I know there's bound to come some trouble to your life
> Reach out to Jesus, hold on tight
> He's been there before and He knows what it's like
> You'll find He's there
>
> There's bound to come some tears up in your eyes
> That ain't nothing to be ashamed of

I know there's bound to come some tears up in your eyes
That ain't no reason to fear

I know there's bound to come some tears up in your eyes
Reach out to Jesus, hold on tight
He's been there before and He knows what it's like
You'll find He's there

Now people say maybe things will get better
People say maybe it won't be long
And people say maybe you'll wake up tomorrow
It'll all be gone

Well, I only know that maybes just ain't enough
When you need something to hold on
There's only one thing that's clear

I know there's bound to come some trouble to your life
But that ain't nothing to be afraid of
I know there's bound to come some tears up in your eyes
That ain't no reason to fear

I know there's bound to come some trouble to your life
Reach out to Jesus, hold on tight
He's been there before and He knows what it's like
You'll find He's there. [138]

Help is best when it comes from the manufacturer. God knows us better than we know ourselves. I often pray, "God, I don't know what I need, but I am convinced that you do. Help me in your wisdom and I will trust you." Sometimes the easy answer from God is different from what I expect the answer to be. Is it easy? It certainly is from God's point of view but from my view it is complicated because I fight with the flesh, culture, and the enemy of my soul. The more I can get to the point of accepting God's way, the easier the answer will be and conversely, the more I resist God's easy answer the longer I will struggle to deal with pain.

As a Pastor, I have had the pain of watching men and women take counsel and discard it like a paper cup, possibly because it seemed too easy for them

---

[138] "Bound to Come Some Trouble," Rich Mullins, from the Album *Never Picture Perfect*, Reunion Records, Brentwood: TN, 1989.

to follow. Maybe you thought I was going to say "difficult". No. The answer was easy, but they believed that it was difficult.

Corrie Ten Boom thought the easy answer was to hate her Nazi captors. After all, they had ravaged her country of the Netherlands and killed many of her family. Corrie revealed her hatred only to be taught by her sister Betsie that the "real" easy answer was to forgive. Betsie along with Corrie were captives in Ravens Bruck concentration camp. Betsie suffered from Anaemia and even though she had fevers, she read a smuggled Bible to her fellow prisoners. She forgave and loved those who treated her cruelly. Betsie told Corrie, "There is no pit so deep that he (Christ) is not deeper still."[139]

In the midst of flea infested barracks and with no physical comforts in sight Betsie Ten Boom told her sister of God's answer to their dilemma. "Give thanks in all circumstances! That's what we can do. We can start right now to thank God for every single thing!"[140]Corrie began to thank God for everything, but Betsie prodded her to give thanks for something so terrible. Fleas. "The fleas! This was too much. Betsie, there's no way even God can make me grateful for a flea. Give thanks in all circumstances. It doesn't say in pleasant circumstances. Fleas are part of this place where God has put us. And so, we stood between piers of bunks and gave thanks for fleas. But this time I was sure Betsie was wrong."[141]

Are there reasons for giving thanks in the middle of horrible circumstances? Yes! No matter how great the problems may be God remains the same. Good. He allows us to suffer, and it may not be pleasant, but he knows, sees, and cares despite what we are feeling. That may be difficult to accept if you're in a concentration camp surrounded by fleas and mistreated by those who do not care about your life. So, you may ask, "why would God allow such horrible pain? This is a legitimate question that only God can fully answer. We have looked at who the creator is and why we can trust him in the worst of situations. Now it's up to each one of us to honestly speak with the creator and exercise faith in him.

"But John, you don't know how hurt I am." Yes, I do! Your pain is real.

---

[139] "The Hiding Place," Corrie ten Boom, with John and Elizabeth Sherrill, New York: NY, Bantam Books, 1971, p.235.

[140] Ibid. 197-99.

[141] Ibid.

Your pain is intense, and you may not see an easy answer although you may have been searching for one. Your pain cannot be eased easily apart from the help of God. I have wept, fasted, and prayed continually for friends, family and even people I don't know, because the easy answer is available, only to see people frequently live out their lives in frustration and pain. It's just not necessary.

Dr. Martin Luther King once wrote, "Darkness cannot drive out darkness; only light can do that. Hate cannot drive out hate; only love can do that."[142] To choose to live with unforgiveness and trouble is senseless because our Creator loves us and can see us through all the trouble that this wicked and sinful world can dish out. God will do even more than see us through the dark tunnel of pain. He will hold our hands through it and will reward the faith that we put in Him.

We spoke of Steve Curtis Chapman's story earlier. He wrote a beautiful song that brought me to tears when I first heard it.

> "I see you sitting over there with your head in your hands
> And the mess life's made of your best laid plans
> You really want to shake your fist
> But you don't know who to blame
> Well you can blame yourself or the man upstairs
> Or the guy on the screen who says he cares
> But all the shame and the blame won't change a thing
> What's done is done
> But grace has just begun
>
> And God's says
> I'm gonna turn it into something different
> I'm gonna turn it into something good
> I'm gonna take all the broken pieces
> And make something beautiful like only I could
> So put it all in the hands of the Father
> Give it up, give it all over to
> The only one who can turn it into
> Something beautiful
> Something really beautiful[143]

---

[142] "Strength to Love," Martin Luther King, Fortress Press, Minneapolis, MN, 1963, p.110.
[143] "Something Beautiful," from the album The Glorious Unfolding, Reunion Records, Brentwood: TN, 2013.

Maybe your hope has gone missing because of the troubles in your life. The words of this song speak life and it turns back the storm clouds. Our prayer for the readers of this book is that each one will see that God loves you and suffering has not changed that fact. Draw close to him by crying out for his help. He will be the one person that will not fail you no matter how bad or how long the trouble lasts.

In the introduction, we quoted Mark Mittelberg in his book, *The Questions Christians Hope No One Will Ask*. In it, he gives excellent guides to navigating through troubles of any kind. Mark writes, "It's encouraging to know that in the midst of even a heavy fog of uncertainty, we can find some 'points of light' to give us direction.

#1 The World is as Jesus predicted
#2 Evil was not created or caused by God
#3 The cause behind most suffering is human
#4 We live in a fallen world
#5 God will finally judge evil
#6 God suffered too
#7 God can bring good out of bad."[144]

We highly recommend reading Mark's book to expand on these points. Later in the same chapter, Mark gives six wonderful examples of how God can bring good things out of bad. You may still be hurting and resistant to reading them, so come back to them when you are ready. They will be there and will be like a drop of water on a parched tongue. He writes that God in His love does things that we just cannot see but benefit by knowing. "He can use pain to deepen our character (Romans 5:3-4), He can use pain to reshape us as his sons and daughters (Hebrews 12:10-11), He can use pain to give us a more spiritual and eternal perspective (2 Corinthians 4:16-18), He can use pain to protect us from ourselves, He can use pain to grab our attention and teach or redirect us in ways that will be important in our lives, He can use pain to lead us to himself."[145]

Pain is not the enemy. In fact, it is most often a friend to everyone. We may try to avoid it with reason, but pain is a blessing. Don't get me wrong. We are not suggesting that anyone seek out pain, rather, we believe that when

---

[144] "The Questions Christians Hope No One Will Ask," Mark Mittelberg, Tyndale House Publishers Inc., Colorado Springs: CO, 2010, p. 114.
[145] Ibid. p.119.

pain does come, it has a purpose that we should understand.

In his best-selling book, coach Tony Dungy wrote concerning his young son, "We thought it was a little odd that Jordan didn't cry when he got his first shots. Then, one afternoon when he was about five months old, I was home alone with him-probably engrossed in a football game, I'm afraid-when he fell off the bed. And didn't cry."[146] After tests, the Dungy's were told that their newborn was missing a gene and could not feel pain like other people do. Not feeling pain would seem to be a relief to us all but it causes more problems than one might think.

Coach Dungy wrote, "Through Jordan, I realized that God allows us to feel pain for a reason: to protect us. God uses many things to show us what to avoid, and painful consequences often teach us lessons quickly. For example, like most kids, Jordan loves cookies. Warm cookies certainly aren't bad for you, at least in moderation. But they are harmful if they're still in the oven. Jordan would reach right in to pull out the piping hot cookie sheet with his bare hands. Then he would begin to eat the cookies without even realizing he was burning his hands and mouth in the process. Even a trip to the emergency room didn't help him understand that he was injuring himself. Lauren and I have had to teach him the consequences of right and wrong, and dangerous activities to protect him. Pain isn't available to him as a teaching tool. Before we had Jordan, I hadn't thought much about the way God uses pain to protect us from further negative consequences down the road. With Jordan, this has become obvious. Pain prompts us to change behavior that is destructive to ourselves or to others. Pain can be a highly effective instructor."[147]

In the book, *Why Suffering*, that we referred to earlier, Vince Vitale encourages the sufferer with a suggestion to the "why" question. "We say we want a world that will never include the possibility of suffering, but do we understand what we ask for? Without the possibility of suffering, practically every great, true story in history would be false. No one would ever have made a significant sacrifice for anyone else. No great moments of forgiveness and reconciliation. No opportunities to stand for justice against injustice. No compassion (because there's nothing to be compassionate

---

[146] "Quiet Strength: The Principles, Practices & Priorities of a Winning Life," Tony Dungy, Tyndale House Publishers, Carol Stream: Ill., p.187, 2007.

[147] Ibid. p. 189.

about). No courage (because no dangerous situations requiring courage). No heroes. No such thing as "laying down one's life for one's friends" (John 15:13). Love itself would be called into question. God could miraculously prevent our actions from ever causing one another to suffer. But if no matter how you spoke to me it sounded good, if no matter how you touched me it felt good, then your words and your touch wouldn't communicate love. There would be no way for me to tell that they were expressions of love rather than of hate. Often, we wish we could just delete the possibility of suffering from this world without changing anything else. But that won't work. We fail to recognize how much good would be lost in losing the possibility of the bad. It is true, I believe that one-day God will bring the suffering of this world to an end. But on that day the celebration will not be that there was never possibility of the bad. It will be far greater than that. It will be that the possibility of evil has been triumphed over, forever defeated by the necessity of the good—God Himself."[148]

No matter how difficult the situation you are facing, even as you read these words, hear, and know that God, the Creator is your answer. He is your easy answer. Pain does not erase the greatness and love of God for you. Reach out to Him and you will not be disappointed by His warm embrace. Like a loving parent, He will gladly be your help and comfort.

The Psalmist David had a confidence in God. This confidence is recorded in Psalm 23, to which we have referred to several times. "The Lord is my shepherd I have all that I need. He lets me rest in green meadows; he leads me beside peaceful streams. He renews my strength. He guides me along right paths, bringing honour to his name. Even when I walk through the darkest valley, I will not be afraid, for you are close beside me" (Psalm 23:1-4 NLT). God will be with you through it all. Accept his easy answers for every situation that you have faced or will ever face.

Knowing that God, the One who created all things and loves us immeasurably, hears us and wisely helps us, gives us reason to be optimistic.

As stated earlier, questions abound when troubles show up. We all frequently ask "why?" We also ask, "How could this happen?" or "When will an answer appear?" Questions are a result of pain and don't always

---

[148] "Why Suffering: Finding Meaning and Comfort When Life Doesn't Make Sense," Ravi Zacharias and Vince Vitale, Faith Words, Brentwood: TN, p.24, 2014.

relieve the pain, but there are some questions that we can ask that will help.

My wife, Carole, wrote these questions that I keep on my desk to bring perspective in challenging moments of life. I want to stimulate you to trust God, not only by reading these questions, but also by questioning yourself when you face trouble.

"Do I believe that God's intentions in my trials are always pure?"

"Is my perspective eternal or focused on my comfort in this life?"

"Am I resentful toward God, blaming him for the times I act sinfully while under pressure?"

"Have I opened myself up to allow God to shine light into my situation?"

"Have I asked him for wisdom to understand my trial?"

"Have I asked him how he wants me to handle my trial?"

"Am I blocking God's light through my doubts, breaking the flow of his character through my character?"

"Is doubt making my situation darker or hiding the goodness of God from the view of those around me?"[149]

We end this book with the encouragement for you to remember that the easy answers that God gives are not divorced from who He is. God interacts with you because He loves and cares for you, even in the trouble you are in. When the answer takes place, let it cause you to draw closer and closer to the One who loves you with an everlasting love. Resist the trap of self-sufficiency when things are going well. Make no mistake, the trap is an extraordinarily strong one that many step in. They may cry out to God for help, and when things are resolved, they look to themselves, things, or the absence of trouble for security. The Creator is the One and Only who sustains, provides, and makes a way for each one of us.

There may be some who do not see the answers come for years. Don't allow time to dictate God's love for you. Patiently wait and believe that the One to whom you cry out, hears you, is working on your behalf, and will bring an easy answer.

---

[149] My wife Carole wrote this list in 2016 to give clear assistance when facing trouble.

You Are Invited

If you don't know Jesus Christ as your personal Lord and Savior, or you want to come to know Him in a deeper understanding and more personal way than you ever have before, then you are invited to pray something like this with us to God:

> Jesus, I believe you are God's Son, and that You died, but death could not hold You because You had no sin to take hold of. You were punished so that I would not have to be. I accept Your gift. Now You have gone to prepare a place in Heaven with Your Father, God, for all those who choose to follow after You. I choose today to follow after You, to be a part of Your Church: The Bride of Christ. I will follow You in sickness and in health, in wealth or poverty; I will follow You to Heaven, and death will never separate us. Teach me to love You above all else, that I may learn to love others as You did, even unto death— Amen.

If this is the first time you have made such a declaration, then welcome to the army of God! If you have decided to re-commit yourself to God, then get ready for the battle. You are going to need a lot of ammo to fight the spiritual forces of darkness, so grab your Bible and load up on God's Word every day. Whichever tour-of-duty you are on, remember that you are never alone. God is with you and He has set an army of believers (or cloud of witnesses[150] around you to love and support you.

Pain should never be experienced alone. Like a fine meal, it's better served when you have someone to share it with. We believe God is the First One who wants to be a part of your circumstance, but we also want to be your support through prayer.

The apostle Paul wrote, "Be patient in trouble, and keep on praying. When God's people are in need, be ready to help them. Always be eager to practice hospitality. Bless those who persecute you. Don't curse them; pray

---

[150] Hebrews 12:2

that God will bless them. Be happy with those who are happy, and weep with those who weep" (Romans 12:12-15).

Another scripture is helpful right now: "Is anyone among you suffering? Then he must pray" (James 4:13). You will struggle. That is a guarantee. Trouble will come. It's a times like that when the best easy answer is to pray.

It would be our honor and joy to support you with prayer. Should you grant us this privilege, please email us with your story so that we can pray for you to receive an Easy Answer.

Send all communication to admin@trulyworship.comand/or cowboyphilosofer@gmx.com

ABOUT
KHARIS PUBLISHING

KHARIS PUBLISHING is an independent, traditional publishing house with a core mission to publish impactful books, and channel proceeds into establishing mini-libraries or resource centers for orphanages in developing countries, so these kids will learn to read, dream, and grow. Every time you purchase a book from Kharis Publishing or partner as an author, you are helping give these kids an amazing opportunity to read, dream, and grow. Kharis Publishing is an imprint of Kharis Media LLC. Learn more at
https://www.kharispublishing.com.

Bibliography

Books

Billy Graham, op cit., Thomas Nelson Inc., Nashville: TN, 2002.

"Choosing to See: A Journey of Struggle and Hope," Mary Beth Chapman, Ellen Santilli Vaughn, Revell Publishing, Oregon City: OR, 2011.

"Funk and Wagnalls New Practical Standard Dictionary," vol. 1, 1949.

"Good God," David Baggett and Jerry L. Walls, Oxford University Press, Oxford: NY, 2011.

Higher Principle Living: A Call to Redemptive Leadership, E. Garry Foreman, WorldCom, Mississauga: ON, 2014.

"Hope for Each Day," Billy Graham, Thomas Nelson Inc., Nashville: TN, 2002.

"Intelligent Thought Management and The Thought Collector," Birdie Wood, Edmonton: AB, 2005.

"I Stand at The Door and Knock," Corrie Ten Boom, Zondervan, Grand Rapids: MI, 2008.

James Dobson, op cit., Tyndale House Publishers, Wheaton: ILL., 2012.

"Jesus Through Middle Eastern Eyes," Kenneth E. Bailey, Intervarsity Press, Downers Grove: ILL., 2008.

"Joni," Joni Eareckson, Zondervan Corp., Grand Rapids: MI, 1977.

"Knowing God," J. I. Packer, Evangelical Press, Welwyn Garden City: UK, 1993.

"Living on The Ragged Edge," Chuck Swindoll, Thomas Nelson, Nashville: TN, 2005.

"Morning and Evening," Charles Spurgeon, Hendrickson Publishers, Peabody: Mass., 1995.

"Our Daily Bread," Grand Rapids: MI, 2016.

"Quiet Strength: The Principles, Practices & Priorities of a Winning Life," Tony Dungy, Tyndale House Publishers, Carol Stream: Ill., 2007.

"Strength to Love," Martin Luther King, Fortress Press, Minneapolis: MN, 1963.

"Surprised by the Voice of God," John S. Deere, Zondervan, Grand Rapids: MI, 1996.

"The Great Gatsby," F. Scott Fitzgerald, Scribner Book Company, NY: NY, 1925.

"The Hiding Place," Corrie ten Boom, with John and Elizabeth Sherrill, Bantam Books, New York: NY, 1971.

"The Journey," Alister McGrath, Random House Inc., NY: NY, 1999.

"The Most Often Asked Questions on Sunday Night Alive", Sheffield Family Life Center, George Westlake, Kansas City: MO, 1997.

"The Purpose Driven Life: What." Rick Warren, Zondervan, Grand Rapids; MI, 2007.

"The Questions Christians Hope No One Will Ask," Mark Mittelberg, Tyndale House Publishers Inc., Colorado Springs: CO, 2010.

"The Zealots," Martin Hengel, T & T Clark, Edinburgh: UK, 1989.

"When God Doesn't Make Sense," James Dobson, Tyndale House Publishers, Wheaton: ILL., 1997.

"While He Lay Dying," Bruce Merz and Lara Merz, Essence Publishing, Belleville: ON, 2014.

"Why Suffering," Ravi Zacharias and Vince Vitale, Faith Words, Brentwood: TN, 2014.

Songs

"Above it All," Jennie Riddle, Travis Ryan, Shawn Craig, 2014, Fair Trade Services.

"And I Will Praise You In the Storm," Mark Hall, Bernie Herms, 2006, Beach Street and Reunion Records.

"Bound to Come Some Trouble," Rich Mullins, 1989, Reunion Records.

"Every Praise," Hezekiah Walker, "Azusa the Next Generation," 2013, RCA Records.

"Can't Keep A Good Man Down," Eddie Carswell, Leonard Ahlstrom, Russ Lee, Benson, 2000.

"God Will Take Care of You," Civilla D. Martin, 1904, Public Domain.

"Hope Has A Name," Philips Craig and Dean from the Album, Above It All, 2014.

"Something Beautiful," Steven Curtis Chapman, Reunion Records, Brentwood: TN, 2013.

"Sometimes He Calms the Storm," Benton Kevin Stokes, Tony W. Wood, Universal Music Publishing Group 1995.

"When Answers Aren't Enough," Scott Wesley Brown and Greg Nelson, 1987, Greg Nelson Music and Pamela Kay Music

Websites

www.allempires.com

www.azquotes.com

www.blogs.tennessean.com

www.blueletterbible.org

www.ca.video.search.yahoo.com

www.cbc.ca

www.ex-christian.net

www.freedomfightersblog.com

www.goodreads.com

www.lumina.bible.org

www.lyrics.com

www.math.ubc.ca

www.psychologytoday.com

www.quotefancy.com

www.sermoncentral.com

www.Sermons.georgeowood.com

www.thefreedictionary.com

www.wikipedia.org

www.youtube.com

CPSIA information can be obtained
at www.ICGtesting.com
Printed in the USA
FSHW022302030621
82022FS